RAYMOND CARVER

A Study of the Short Fiction

Also available in Twayne's Studies in Short Fiction Series

Twayne's Studies in Short Fiction

Gordon Weaver, General Editor
Oklahoma State University

RAYMOND CARVER
© *Lewis Thompson*

RAYMOND CARVER

A Study of the Short Fiction

Ewing Campbell
Texas A&M University

TWAYNE PUBLISHERS • NEW YORK
Maxwell Macmillan Canada • Toronto
Maxwell Macmillan International • New York Oxford Singapore Sydney

Twayne's Studies in Short Fiction Series, No. 31

Twayne Publishers ˙   Maxwell Macmillan Canada, Inc.
Macmillan Publishing Company ˰   1200 Eglinton Avenue East
866 Third Avenue   Suite 200
New York, NY 10022   Don Mills, Ontario M3C 3N1

Macmillan Publishing Company is part of the Maxwell Communication
Group of Companies.

Library of Congress-in-Publication Data

Campbell, Ewing.
     Raymond Carver : a study of the short fiction / Ewing Campbell.
       p.   cm. — (Twayne's studies in short fiction series; no. 31)
     Includes bibliographical references and index.
     ISBN 0-8057-8300-8
       1. Carver, Raymond—Criticism and interpretation.   2. Short story.
     I. Title.   II. Series: Twayne's studies in short fiction; no. 31
     PS3553.A7894Z58   1992
     813'.54—dc20   91-32991
                                                                    CIP

10 9 8 7 6 5 4 3 2 1

70740

Contents

Preface

The crucial gesture of criticism, if not the essential, is finding the necessary distance between the critic and the work to be judged. It is always difficult to attain the critical distance required for any lasting assessment, but by no means impossible. The difficulty increases when one addresses literature that is contemporary with the assessment, especially if the work under consideration comes from an individual recognized during his life as one of the premiere writers. Such is the situation for anyone confronting Raymond Carver's fiction during the last decade of the twentieth century, and it is an inviting challenge.

While too little time has passed for his staying power to have been properly tested, Carver's concise interpretations of American malaise and despair seem firmly in place. There is already a body of evidence to support the position his reputation enjoys. That body of evidence, consisting of both facts and generally held perceptions, includes a great deal of critical and popular recognition. For example, his work has been translated into more than 20 languages. He received a Guggenheim Fellowship, two National Endowment for the Arts Fellowships, a Mildred and Harold Strauss Living Award, and the Levinson Prize, in addition to being elected to the American Academy and Institute of Arts and Letters. His fiction has been included more than a dozen times in *Prize Stories: The O. Henry Awards*, *The Best American Short Stories*, or *The Pushcart Prizes*, and his collections of short fiction were nominated for the National Book Award, the Pulitzer Prize, and the National Book Critics Circle Award.

These are the facts. His perceived contributions to the genre of short fiction are equally impressive. In the current revival of American realism, he is credited with resuscitating the short story as an artistically and commercially legitimate form. His successes suggest that it is once again possible for young writers to concentrate on short stories with some hope of getting published. Indeed, publishers are now issuing collections of fiction as first books by unknown writers.

Credited with founding the minimalist school of fiction, he has been a strong influence on young writers. Not since Ernest Hemingway has there been a more imitated American author. Even if the perceptions are inaccurate, *What We Talk about When We Talk about Love* remains the standard by which minimalist fiction is measured, and his role as the extender of a modernist tradition that stretches from Chekhov through James Joyce to Ernest Hemingway (each influenced Carver) and beyond is significant.

This role necessitates an examination of literary context, with special attention paid to the patterns occurring within individual stories and repeated from one story to the next. Beneath Carver's so-called plain style, readers can find a keen literary interpretation of a particular time and place, universal themes, and a cultural mythology that expands the context of his insistently local stories.

Such are the working conditions for anyone who looks into the short fiction of Raymond Carver. Each story is like the paneling of a cedar-lined closet: scuff its surface, and it never fails to release some of its essence. Therein lies the pleasure, emotional and intellectual. For to examine Carver's compositions as reshaped experience, whether of blue-collar despair or of redeeming insight, is to experience the life that takes shape before the mind's eye. Any understanding of the composed scene and events forms a dialogue with the author, and out of such intercourse we come to know ourselves and to grasp our world a little more clearly.

In scrutinizing this experience, we inevitably take a work's form into consideration because its shape is inseparable from its essence. With that in mind, I extend the notion of form to the complete body of fiction, then break this larger shape into manageable phases for practical purposes, calling them phases of apprenticeship, breakthrough, maturity, and mastery. I identify each phase with the collection that matches it in order of publication: *Will You Please Be Quiet, Please?* (1976), *What We Talk about When We Talk about Love* (1981), *Cathedral* (1984), and *Where I'm Calling From* (1988), which I quote from whenever possible. Passages from other sources either do not appear in *Where I'm Calling From* or do not appear there in the form I wish to quote.

The scope of this work is limited to analyzing the fiction and does not attempt to join the events of Carver's life with the composition of individual stories. While his recurring themes and characteristic topics are inseparable from his life and obsessions, that potentially rich vein must be left for the biographer to mine. However, even without this significant material, there remain important configurations of myth and archetype, motifs of the grotesque, of otherness, the reconciling factor of characters imagining others' lives, and the opposite—characters failing to make the imaginative leap that will connect them with others.

These configurations and motifs are pervasive in Carver's work. They can be found in his earliest work and in the stories written at the end of his life. In "Errand," the final story of Carver's last collection, the juxtaposition of Madame Chekhov and the young waiter—one making the leap of imagination as the other stands rooted in the literal and the trivial—is prefigured in "Fat," which opens his first collection of short fiction, *Will You Please Be Quiet, Please?* (1976). "Pastoral," composed at the beginning of his career, and "Blackbird Pie," at the end, share a deep symbolic concern with emasculation. Religious iconography exists in Carver's work as early as "Nobody Said Anything" and as late as "Intimacy."

The critical challenge is to plumb a deceptive art that depends on apparent simplicity, purports to be straightforward and functional, and insists that the surface is all there is. That challenge is accepted every time we attempt to stop the perpetual motion of a literary work and bring the shifting elements into focus. Vague gestures, unspoken or misspoken words, contrary implications—these work against the desired stability of criticism, and the task becomes increasingly difficult when the work is truncated, indirect, seemingly detached from its creator.

Nevertheless, different versions of the same story can furnish evidence for the most indirect intention, and Carver published versions of the same stories in *Furious Seasons* (1977) and *What We Talk about When We Talk about Love* (1981), the breakthrough volume in which he perfects his minimalist idiom. By publishing a large enough number of these variations, he leaves instructive patterns that readers can use to good advantage.

With notable exceptions in his late fiction, Carver peopled his fiction with fringe figures—unemployed salesmen, oppressed waitresses, drunken motel clerks, adulterers, disturbed mill workers—which led inevitably to characteristic topics of alcoholism, infidelity, insomnia, and despair. A justification of the commonplace finds itself in his determination to represent the lives of these fringe figures honestly, however unpalatable that portrayal might be. It is a narrow, inglorious story of America, but an important one that needs recording, and it found an uncompromising chronicler in Raymond Carver.

After the success of his second commercial collection, *What We Talk About* (1981), Carver—perhaps reacting to the minimalist tag—began to take a more generous and open approach to his characters and themes. In *Cathedral* (1984), his most mature work at the time of its publication, characters representing articulate, affluent America find a voice, as do themes of redemption and insight. We also encounter a drift toward popular forms, sentiment, allegory, and myth, as Carver constructs a transitional work that bridges the chasm between minimalism and the bold fiction of the last volume.

Some of the new fiction in *Where I'm Calling From*, his last collection, reveals a mastery of forms Carver had ignored for decades. The last two stories mark absolutely new boundaries for him and offer the promise of a bold new path, a promise subverted not by any loss of skill, but by his death, which came at the height of his creative powers.

Now that the responsibility has shifted in Carver's case from creation to criticism, the process of patient, measured evaluation begins in earnest. It is a process that is always subject to the vicissitudes of popular and critical tastes, always at peril because of biases, but it is no less valuable in spite of its flaws. Readers are urged to keep in mind one principle: that critical value lies not in the contradictory answers to questions of meaning, but in the questioning itself. Analysis is best not as an end in itself, but when it brings pressure to bear on the object of attention.

Acknowledgments

I wish to acknowledge the support of the Fulbright Program and the National University of Córdoba, Argentina, through which I was able to refine and test the ideas of this study in the form of lectures.

"On Writing," from *Fires*, by Raymond Carver, © 1983. Reprinted by permission of Capra Press, Santa Barbara, California.

"An Interview with Raymond Carver," from *Alive and Writing: Interviews with American Authors of the 1980s*, conducted and edited by Larry McCaffery and Sinda Gregory, 1987. Reprinted by permission of University of Illinois Press. © 1987 by the Board of Trustees of the University of Illinois.

"Finding the Words: The Struggle for Salvation in the Fiction of Raymond Carver" by Kathleen Westfall Shute first appeared in *Hollins Critic* 24 no. 5 1987: 1–9. © 1987 *Hollins Critic*. Reprinted by permission.

"Raymond Carver and the Menace of Minimalism" by Mark A. R. Facknitz first appeared in *CEA Critic* 52, no. 1-2 (Fall 1989–Winter 1990): 62–73. © 1990 *CEA Critic*. Reprinted by permission.

"Now You See Him, Now You Don't, Now You Do Again: The Evolution of Raymond Carver's Minimalism" by Adam Meyer first appeared in *Critique* 30 (1989): 239–251. © 1989 *Critique*. Reprinted by permission.

Frontispiece sketch of Raymond Carver by Lewis Thompson. © by Lewis O. Thompson.

Part 1

THE SHORT FICTION

Apprenticeship: *Will You Please Be Quiet, Please?*

> Everything I have written will be forgotten in a few years. But the paths I have traced will remain intact and secure, and there lies my merit.
>
> —Anton Chekhov

Prophetic, perceptive words indeed: "But the paths I have traced will remain intact and secure, and there lies my merit."[1] For a hundred years, the literary paths Chekhov traced have led strong writers from different nations to discoveries that helped shape and describe their respective cultures. The indirect, understated form he, as much as anyone, helped develop was the prototype of the modern short story. American writers in particular have followed these paths, but none as consistently and successfully as Raymond Carver.

Apprenticeships are usually thought of as the individual's struggle to master the methods of a discipline or an art, the search for a voice, the coming to terms with experience, the absence of maturity. With some, however, the early years are marked by a sureness and control that belie the individual's relative inexperience. Among short story writers, we can point to the early published fiction of James Joyce and Ernest Hemingway as examples of such precocity.

Raymond Carver's first stories demonstrate, in a similar fashion, the unusual sureness of a young writer who has already found his voice and the motifs that will preoccupy him for the rest of his life. What was there at the beginning was still there at the end, although the vigorous style had evolved from precociousness to mastery by then. Of immediate concern, however, are the stories that frame the apprentice period. "Pastoral" (1963) appeared in *Western Humanities Review*, and Carver said in *"The Paris Review* Interview" that it was his first published story.[2] Although he left it out of his first collection, he did include it in *Furious Seasons and Other Stories* (1977) and later in *Fires: Essays, Poems, Stories* (1984), as "The Cabin."

"Will You Please Be Quiet, Please?" is the last story of his first collection and gives its title to that volume. Selected for *The Best American Short Stories* anthology of 1967, it brought him national recognition and critical attention; for a long time, it was his best-known story.

"Pastoral" and "Will You Please Be Quiet, Please?" are important not only because they form the boundaries of the fiction in his initial phase, but also because they are the clearest examples of the debt Carver owed to James Joyce. While the kinship with Chekhov's and Hemingway's fiction is often noted, Carver's relation to Joyce's early fiction was rarely, if ever, emphasized during Carver's life and has apparently been overlooked by critics since his death, although he cited *Dubliners* as an influential work (Simpson, 207). The notable element in the relation between these two diametric writers—one expansive, the other constrictive—is not the debt, but that Carver was able to transform the Joycean readings within his experience, inclinations, limitations, and abilities to produce a quality indisputably his own, and to do so at a relatively early age. We now recognize that quality as his signature and pay tribute to it by creating a red-letter heading, *the Carveresque*, under which a distinct category of fiction is classified.

"Pastoral" ("The Cabin")

Reprinted as "The Cabin" in *Fires*, "Pastoral" is not a story that will be taught often in college literature courses; nor is it among the fictions Carver chose for *Where I'm Calling From: New and Selected Stories*. Nevertheless, it is indispensable for tracing Carver's development as a writer working within the tradition of the modern short story, which is epiphanous in theme and method and truncated in structure.

Although epiphanous fiction existed before James Joyce, Joyce is its acknowledged master in English. It was he who appropriated *epiphany* from Greek mythology and Christian religion for his theory of art, using the term to designate the sudden revelation of a situation's or a character's true nature. In his poetics, the insight arrived through word, gesture, deed, or object and caused the reader or character to see matters in a new light. Carver's use conforms with Joyce's.

Half a century passed between the publication of Joyce's *Dubliners* and the time Carver began to publish his stories, time enough for the new to become established. Within this tradition, Hemingway had already shown the world that serious fiction could be written about hunting and fishing, activities that were also important to Carver. As he said in the *Paris Review* interview, "In those days, I went fishing in this creek that was not too far from our house. A little later, I started hunting ducks and geese and upland game. That's what excited me in those days, hunting and fishing. That's what made a dent in my emotional life, and that's what I wanted to write about" (Simpson, 190). Later in "An Interview with Raymond Carver," conducted by Larry McCaffery and Sinda Gregory, he expressed the same idea: "I began writing by wanting to write about those things like hunting and fishing that played a real part in my emotional life. And I did write about nature quite a lot in my early poems and stories: you can find it in many of the stories in *Furious Seasons* and in some of the ones in *Will You Please Be Quiet, Please?*"[3] With such distinguished precedent, he did not hesitate to take the familiar activities and codes of the outdoors as material for his first nationally published story.

Mr. Harrold of "Pastoral" returns to the Castlerock hunting and fishing camp where he once experienced happiness. He notes a Frederic Remington reproduction depicting Indians hunting hanging above the counter of the café. He sees a vandalized shed on the grounds and knows that it is the handiwork of individuals ungoverned by ordinances or custom. The next morning he goes fishing, pushing through the underbrush and woods with his rod held out like a lance, recalling that he had acted in the same manner when he was young, imagining himself in the lists jousting with foes. While fishing he sees a wounded doe pursued by the vandals who have shot her. They ask if he has seen her. His response is a quixotic challenge to the barbarians who do not know or care about the traditional codes of hunting. In the unexpected confrontation between the imaginary good old days and the vulgar reality of the present, he stands like a stag brought to bay by the hounds and defiantly asks who wants to know. The youth with the gun points it at Mr. Harrold's lower body, and he suddenly feels the chill of the cold river. His throat goes dry. He experiences an uncontrollable yawning, an emotional manifestation called *chasmus hystericus*, and in confusion, he rushes back to the cabin, losing his rod somewhere along the way. Back at the cabin he senses that he has lost something heroic, which existed only in his fantasies and nostalgic reveries of the past.

Expressed this way, the details establish the conflict between Mr. Harrold, who likes order, and his antagonists, who are the enemies of order. The threat replaces his romantic self-image with the fear most people feel when in danger and results in his disillusionment. However, the implications of the events, given the language and images

Carver employs in the story, signal a theme that extends beyond individual interest to expose the general futility of nostalgia and self-deception as therapy for malaise. By noting the echoes and connotations of strategically placed words and images that create a pattern, we can discover the hidden situation, which the superficial conflict emphasizes and resolves.

The name of the protagonist announces the milieu within which everything occurs and evokes a long list of Norse and Saxon heroes who, like King Harold at the Battle of Hastings, ended their lives in defeat. This initial heroic resonance is reinforced by the name of the camp, Castlerock, and by the Frederic Remington reproduction, which portrays lurching buffaloes pursued by Indians with drawn bows, so that a relation between the words and images begins to take shape. Whether Mr. Harrold thinks of Remington's other favorite subject— the cowboy as knight-errant engaged in violent struggle to the death— or not, the reader is certainly meant to recognize that the cowboys, Indians, and buffaloes mythologized by Remington are as much a part of the vanished past as heroic kings and jousting knights.

We know from Carver's response in the McCaffery-Gregory interview that he meant for the objects in his fiction to function as more than mere setting: "This might mean including as part of the setting a television or a table or a felt-tipped pen lying on a desk, but if these things are going to be introduced into the scene at all, they shouldn't be inert. . . . You want to give them some weight, connecting these things to the lives around them. I see the objects as playing a 'role' in the stories" (McCaffery, 72).

By recognizing the roles of connected images in the first paragraphs of "Pastoral," one can hardly miss the parallels with chivalric times, codes of honor, courage, the sense of a lost better life; and as the story advances, other elements contribute to the heroic effect. For instance, Harrold encounters the vandalized shed, which conjures images of the Vandals and expands the web of chivalric images. By means of the damage, he first learns about those he must later face, a device that helps to prepare for his confrontation with the enemies of order. Moreover, Carver's connotative diction (exemplified in the use of such words as *lance* and *lists*) and Mr. Harrold's fantasies about the past work through a process of accretion to create an idealized self-image. We can see this vividly at work in the following passage from "The Cabin": "He held the rod by its big reel, tucked up under his arm like a lance.

Sometimes, back when he was a kid and had gone into a remote area to fish for two or three days at a time, hiking in by himself, he'd carried his rod like this, even when there was no brush or trees, maybe just a big green meadow. Those times he would imagine himself waiting for his opponent to ride out of the trees on a horse" (*Fires*, 133).

The more we see of this self-image, the more we apprehend his sense of isolation. At some point in the story, we recall that his wife has not accompanied him, that she did not share his taste for Chinese landscapes, that he, like Byron's Childe Harold, has embarked on a solitary pilgrimage. And we begin to realize that he sees himself alone against a hostile world, much like a knight on a quest.

But Harrold is undergoing more than delusions of knight-errantry. His manhood is at stake, for we can see symbolic links between his self-image and masculinity. The fishing rod functions as both the weapon of knighthood and the emblem of male virility. Not content to rely on symbolism, Carver wants his reader to experience the palpable threat of emasculation when the vandal points his weapon at Harrold's lower body. Spared the actual loss, he rushes back to the cabin, where Carver returns to symbolism to make his point, for during Harrold's flight, he has lost his rod in symbolic emasculation. Although no overt epiphany occurs in "The Cabin," the *Western Humanities Review* version contains Harrold's confused realization that he has lost something heroic, exposing the vanity and impotence of his nostalgic yearning for a heroic past. Significantly, the lost rod appears in all published versions of the story.

If the discrepancy between the vulgar present and nostalgic yearning for a heroic past applied only to Mr. Harrold, the story would have its interest, but would lack the significance we have come to expect from serious fiction. The value of the story resides in its projection of a world pertinent to all. It presents an internal conflict that forces the character to reinterpret his world and himself along more judicious lines. At the same time, the reader is allowed to experience and interpret, both before and during the moment of crisis without intrusive commentary by the author, the character's impotence, manifest in his psychological paralysis at the end and in the symbolism of his emasculation.

Like Joyce, Carver included moments of spiritual fullness and revelations of a character's folly or blindness. Readers of Joyce's short fiction will see the similarities between "Pastoral" or "The Cabin" and "Araby," stories in which the protagonists' idealized visions of heroic worlds are subverted by epiphanies of vulgar reality. The epiphanous technique, as practiced by Joyce and Carver, can have diametric effects, engendering in the reader either a sense of discovery or a sense of resentment toward the author if the unstated intention remains ungrasped. It is rewarding when the discovery occurs, but the threatening alternative renders much modern fiction, despite its dominance in this century, burdensome and consequently unsuitable for most popular and many literary publications.

The difficulty accounts for part of the hostility among critics and readers toward such fiction, whether written by Joyce, Hemingway, or Carver. Mark Facknitz, citing Frank O'Connor's volatile reaction to Hemingway's indirect stories, illustrates this attitude: "In *The Lonely Voice*, Frank O'Connor confesses that he is frequently exasperated by Hemingway's limited scope,"[4] which is attributed to a technique without subject. However, the hostility cannot be attributed to the technique alone, for the substance of Carver's fiction, his fictional milieu and portrayal of unpleasant experience—Mr. Harrold's disillusionment, for example—must bear part of the responsibility.

"Nobody Said Anything"

Carver chose to begin *Where I'm Calling From* (1988) with "Nobody Said Anything." Like "Pastoral," it makes use of fishing, and that shared material, along with the story's placement in the final collection, which links the two stories chronologically, is good reason for following a discussion of "Pastoral" with an examination of "Nobody Said Anything." As an editor's note states "the stories in this collection are arranged, generally, in chronological order."[5]

Gone are the heroic allusions of the first story. The language shifts as Carver moves toward mastering his own voice, but in his switch from the third person of "Pastoral" to a first-person narrator confused by adult tensions and his own sexuality, Carver revisits the situation of "Araby."

"Nobody Said Anything" is a subtle, understated realization of a small triumph. If the epiphanous moment in "Pastoral" is an example of unpalatable experience, the comparable moment in "Nobody Said Anything" is an epiphany of spiritual fullness, in spite of its smallness. In Carver's world, small triumphs are magnified by their intensity, but often missed because of his indirection. "Nobody Said Anything" is the earliest clear anticipation of "A Small, Good Thing," his popular and critical success of later years, in its exploitation of religious icon-ography. Prefiguring the eucharistic conclusion of "A Small, Good Thing," Carver fashions a symbolic redemption from the realistic de-tails and secular situation of a boy's struggle with familial conflict. The family is coming apart, and as the parents quarrel, the young narrator is forced to observe this disintegration without understanding it or hav-ing the means to stop it. On several occasions, he seeks to communi-cate with someone only to find himself without words or with others who refuse to listen. Hearing his parents bickering one morning and his mother crying, he wakes his brother, hoping that George will speak up and stop the quarrel, but George merely says, "I don't care" (*Where*, 3).

Pretending to be sick, the narrator stays home from school and at-tempts to discover the mysteries of sex by snooping around in his par-ents' room, searching for condoms, going through their drawers, and trying to read sexual secrets on the label of a Vaseline jar. He wants to experience sex, but must settle for uninformed fantasies and repeated masturbatory occasions. Unsatisfied, restless, and not finding answers, he decides to go fishing and, on his way to Birch Creek, is given a ride by a lady. He imagines a sexual encounter with her and wants to prop-osition her, but cannot bring himself to do so. After she lets him out, he chides himself for his failure to think of all that comes to him now that it is too late.

At the creek, he meets a boy who helps him catch a fish that is striking in size and color, which he divides and shares with the boy. This fish becomes the narrator's pretext for interrupting the quarrel between his mother and father upon his return home. What his brother would not do as the story opens, and a pan burning on the stove cannot do now, he achieves with his half of the grotesque fish.

Foisting the creature on his mother and father, he deflects their fury from each other to himself as they order him to get rid of it. Instead he goes out and looks into the creel at what once appeared strange and ugly, but now looks silver under the light. Lovingly, triumphantly, be-cause the fish has provided the temporary means to stop his parents' fighting, he lifts and embraces it: "I held him. I held that half of him" (*Where*, 16).

Alone, not understanding the source of family tensions and without the means of discovering them, the narrator feels trapped and helpless. Bound by his incomplete understanding, the unbearable bickering of his parents, and a situation of no one listening or communicating, his world begins to present itself to him in contrasting images of imprisonment and freedom, mirroring his feelings and desires. When he looks at the other boy, he sees the face of a trapped rat, and when they catch the fish, that image recurs. Like the people of the story, the fish is not about to get away, but the narrator could be speaking of himself when he says, "He's not going anyplace. There's no place for him to go" (*Where*, 10). At the same time, airplanes taking off and landing at the airport suggest the freedom he desires.

Further evidence of such desires can be found in his antisocial behavior, his disregard for rules, and his unrealized fantasies. First, he begins a series of violations, manipulating his distracted mother with the lie that he is ill in order to stay out of school, stealing her cigarettes, disobeying her. When he goes to the creek, he disregards restrictions, climbing through fences and ignoring keep-out signs, acting out symbolic gestures of crossing boundaries. Unsatisfied by television and escapist fiction, he smokes, masturbates, and searches his parents' bedroom, as if sex is behind the trouble in the family and as soon as he knows the answers the trouble will cease to exist. His adolescent sexual preoccupation contributes to his troubled emotions, as do the contradictory signals he receives from others.

Just as no one in the family listens, no one speaks up about unhealthy situations. The brother's refusal is only the first example. After directing the narrator to keep the television off, his mother sees him watching it, but remains silent. The orchard smudge pots pollute the air and leave their residue in the characters' noses, "but nobody said anything. They said the smudging kept the young pears from freezing, so it was all right" (*Where*, 6).

Carver is not usually credited with hopeful themes before the publication of *Cathedral*, and yet, he actually wrote and published a number of stories built on spiritual communion early in his career, as the transformation of the grotesque fish into an image of silver beauty at the end of "Nobody Said Anything" affirms. This transfiguration is essential to the story. Just as Mr. Harrold's lost fishing rod possesses a symbolic and psychological value beyond its ordinary function, the fish is transported from the secular to the spiritual realm, where it becomes more than a memorable image or a prop that brings the parents' fight to an end. As Larry McCaffery and Sinda Gregory assert, the "initial impression of verisimilitude gives way to an unsettling recognition that things are not simply as they appear. Or rather, that things are *more* than what they appear, for often commonplace objects in his stories—

a broken refrigerator, cars, cigarettes, a bottle of beer or whiskey—become in Carver's hands more than realistic props in realistic stories, but powerful, emotionally charged signifiers in and of themselves" (McCaffery, 62).

Let us subject this assertion to rigorous scrutiny. The first question might be, Is the fish necessary for a spiritual transfiguration or can it be replaced by any other object without loss to the story? If so, it is hardly indispensable. If, however, it performs a function without which the story would be less or other than it is, a strong argument exists for the status of "emotionally charged signifier." Searching for significance unique to the fish, one soon discovers that the *ichthys*—Greek for fish, a symbol consisting of two facing curved lines overlapping at one end, and an anagram of the phrase *I*esous *CH*ristos, *TH*eou *Y*ios, *S*oter (Jesus Christ, Son of God, Saviour)—is one of the oldest and most persistent symbols of redemption. Through the intervening agency of the ichthys, rather than some other object, the narrator halts his parents' fight and reestablishes familial equilibrium. At the same time, the act introduces a mythic quality that ramifies the realism of the story and invests it with both allegorical content and a universal theme of the spiritual.

Although the details reveal themselves little by little until the finished web hangs in all its intricacy before us, within the story's sequence of figures and scenes, a perception passes across our line of sight as we read and is concentrated in the controlling image of the fish. As readers, we remake the scenes and figures, perhaps with difficulty, until slowly we begin to uncover the connections that complete the pattern and give it meaning. In the process of interpretation, we see that Carver is interested in something more than his familiar activity of fishing.

He desires an object imbued with meaning, a scene of greater duration than an interrupted squabble, one whose afterimage lingers in the mind's eye long after the story closes. With great subtlety, he finds those qualities in a cherished symbol made common and realistic in its presentation. Thus, we see that Carver's method of investing ordinary objects with emotional power relies on cultural traditions, whether the sacred traditions of Christianity, Freudian interpretations of sexuality, or the popular mythologizing of Frederic Remington. As the method becomes clearer, readers are less likely to be frustrated by Carver's indirection.

"Fat"

In "Fat," certain, but not all, characteristics particular, if not exclusive, to Carver begin to emerge—the highly stylized repetition, exemplified here in the phrase *I say:* "Go right ahead, I say. A person has to be comfortable, I say" (*Where*, 50); encounters with the grotesque other; imagination of another life, often contrasted with a failure of imagination; and the obsessive personality.

The waitress-narrator opens her report of a conversation she is having with her friend Rita by saying, "I am sitting over coffee and cigarettes at my friend Rita's and am telling her about it" (*Where*, 48). The hovering *it*, another commonplace of Carver's style, refers in this instance to the narrator's encounter with an obese customer. He has come in and embarked on a gargantuan feast, eating large portions with the gusto of someone at a banquet. His size and unrestrained appetite are extraordinary and unforgettable. During the course of relating details of her serving him and of their conversation, she describes the effect of this experience on her imagination, especially the effect it has on her self-image during sex. The blurred lines between the imagined other and the self, actually the merging of the two, become resources for Carver's characters, ways of imposing structure on their experiences, and finally hints of a vaguely altered future.

Rita's dim reaction to the details is perfunctory. "That's a funny story," she says (*Where*, 52), but the narrator can see Rita has no idea what to make of the experience. Because Rita's failure to understand depresses the narrator, she decides to leave matters there, regretting that she has gone into as much detail as she has.

By the time Carver wrote "Fat," he was marking out his territory with one of his most persistently recurring motifs, encounters with the grotesque. It is a brief story, but one rich in topics of considerable import: namely, the concept of grotesque realism and its leading themes—the material body, unrestrained appetites, growth, and brimming abundance; the principle of self-discovery in the other, with its implications of change; and human experience created in the alchemy of the imagination, including its opposite, the absence of any imagined experience.

Three features strike the narrator when she first sees her obese customer: the man's size, his strange habit of using the all-inclusive *we* in his speech, and his fingers: "When I stop at the table near his to see to the old couple, I first notice the fingers. They look three times the size of a normal person's fingers—long, thick, creamy fingers. . . . God, Rita, but those were fingers" (*Where*, 48). These elements have been examined extensively in *Rabelais and His World* by the provocative Russian theorist of the novel, Mikhail Bakhtin.

According to Bakhtin, the grotesque is typically manifested in exaggerated images of the belly, nose, and other bodily protuberances, such as the fingers, and is positive in nature.[6] That characterization agrees with Carver's portrayal, and the fat man's inclusive way of speaking lends itself to Bakhtin's interpretation that "the bodily element is deeply positive . . . something universal, representing all the people" (Bakhtin, 19).

As notable as the fingers are, the narrator senses, without articulating it precisely, that the way people treat otherness is an important part of her experience. Recounting one of her coworkers comments, "Who's your fat friend? He's really a fatty," she tells Rita, "Now that's part of it. I think that is really part of it" (*Where*, 49). The undefined *it* she evokes here is the principle of difference. Only a small, initial movement toward recognizing her own difference in the fat man, the remark suggests a link between the two. The link is reinforced when she tells the customer that she too eats without restraint, although in her case she cannot gain weight.

After her boyfriend's derisive remark, "Some fatty" (*Where*, 51), she puts her hand on her stomach and wonders what would happen if she had children who were obese. By the time she and Rudy are going through the motions of sex, the gestation of identity is recognizable in her transformed imagination: "But here is the thing. When he gets on me, I suddenly feel I am fat. I feel I am terrifically fat, so fat that Rudy is a tiny thing and hardly there at all" (*Where*, 51–52).

Identification with the other is foreshadowed in the restaurant by the man's appreciation of food. His eating is solitary, but there can be no question about its festive quality, as manifest in his good cheer and large appetite. His attitude points to the narrator's change in perception, for the feast has always been associated with moments of renewal and a festive perception of the world. The intrusion into her life of the customer, exuding inclusiveness and zest, demonstrates how random initial factors can cause essential variables to dance in the imagination, bringing about an unexpected change in the subject.

Her renewal, although recognizable and foreshadowed, must not be viewed as finished or in any way static, for she is in the fluid state of becoming. Her last words indicate the force of this belief: "My life," she says, "is going to change. I feel it" (*Where*, 52). Her conviction expresses an existential leap of faith.

One might argue reasonably that such a realization is, in and of itself, evidence that a change has already taken place, but there is an additional aspect to consider: the link between compulsion (the man's) and leaps of the imagination (the narrator's). The combination often finds its expression in the acts and works of artists. Kafka's "A Hunger Artist," for example, combines the artist and the compulsive personality in a work of fiction.

Kafka's hunger artist's dying words ("Because I have to fast, I can't help it"[7]) are worth thinking about in conjunction with the words of Carver's eating artist: "If we had our choice, no. But there is no choice" (*Where*, 51). This denial sounds so reminiscent of the hunger artist's that to ignore the similarity is to ignore literary precedent, for the artist as other, as grotesque, or as someone with great unrestrained appetites is not new.

The source of Carver's eating artist who has no choice is visible in its opposition to Kafka's hunger artist who had no choice but to fast. As Jonathan Culler stresses in *Structuralist Poetics*, "If the text presents two items—characters, situations, objects, actions—in a way which suggests opposition," possibilities of substitution and variation reveal themselves.[8] Since each theme has its antithesis, every theme is compounded the moment it is known. Culler's principle of opposition and antithesis provides a foundation on which to begin, for Carver's story is shaped by Kafka's earlier narrative, antithetically. He complicates and enriches his story by providing what is missing in Kafka's story: someone who intuits and identifies with the artistic compulsion. In this instance, the narrator's recognition of her own unsatisfied appetites is a manifestation of the creative act, just as Rita's failure to identify with the narrator is an example of its opposite. Whereas the hunger artist's otherness exists unshared, the narrator of "Fat" recognizes her own otherness in Carver's eating artist, thus sharing his condition.

"Neighbors"

Carver was writing excellent fiction during the years that included "Fat," fiction serious in content, professional in execution, but was not publishing his stories in large-circulation commercial magazines, at least not until he received a letter of rejection from Gordon Lish, the fiction editor at *Esquire*. According to Carver, Lish asked to see other stories: "I was writing a short story that I'd called 'The Neighbors.' I finally finished the story and sent it off to Lish. A letter came back almost immediately telling me how much he liked it, that he was changing the title to 'Neighbors,' that he was recommending to the magazine that the story be purchased. It was purchased, it did appear, and nothing, it seemed to me, would ever be the same" (*Fires*, 30). Other stories were accepted by *Esquire* following the publication of "Neighbors" (1971), and Carver's career did take one of its important turns.

"Neighbors," with its portrait of shared imagination and the characters' sense of difference and exclusion, fits the mold of "Fat." That portrait begins with the Millers' self-image and their belief that the Stones, who live across the hall, lead fuller and more exciting lives than they. However, one day, opportunity presents itself in the form of a responsibility.

Charged with the neighborly care of the Stones' apartment, cat, and plants while they are away, Bill and Arlene Miller find their lives altered by their separate forays across the hall. With an opportunity to examine the objects of that other, fuller life and experience it vicariously, Bill begins to look into the Stones' private places, to sample their intimate articles. His voyeurism produces the desired effect, an excitement that has been absent from his life, but his transformation remains unshared until Arlene, noting the change in him, follows his example and makes her own stimulating trip across the hall.

Bill Miller's behavior consists of two kinds of endeavors: pointedly taking in substances that belong to the Stones and inserting himself into their spaces and belongings. The combination results in increased sexual activity at home.

In the first category, one finds several instances that are notable. First, he makes a point of inhaling their air: "Bill took a deep breath as he entered the Stones' apartment. The air was already heavy and it was vaguely sweet" (*Where*, 66). Then he filches Harriet Stone's pills from the medicine cabinet and a pack of cigarettes from the nightstand. He drinks from the Chivas Regal bottle in the liquor cabinet. Air, pills, tobacco smoke, and alcohol—all of them elements taken into the body. Upon returning to his apartment stimulated, he touches Arlene's breasts, urging her to bed.

The next afternoon, a mere glance at the door across the hall is sufficient for him to initiate sex. Afterward, he crosses to the neighbors' apartment and repeats with variation the acts of the previous visit: "He sniffed some celery, took two bites of cheddar cheese, and chewed on an apple as he walked into the bedroom" (*Where*, 67). Arlene's knock on the door prevents further adventures, but that night, they make love again.

The other category of enclosing himself in their belongings can be seen in his attraction to their apartment, which seems cooler and darker than his own, and his getting into their bed, which leads to masturbation: "He lay for a while with his eyes closed, and then he moved his hand under his belt" (*Where*, 68). He dons Jim Stone's vacation clothes; he tries on a business suit, tie, and wing-tip shoes before regarding the effect in the mirror as if imagining himself in the other's role. Still not satisfied, he changes into Harriet's intimate articles, skirt, and burgundy blouse.

The role-playing is a solitary exercise. Arlene sees only the effects of Bill's trips—his increased ardor and his appetite—but they are not lost on her. His change, brought about by the vicarious behavior, is puzzling enough for her to ask, "What's gotten into you?" (*Where*, 67). She can see that his transformation follows the trips to the Stones' apartment. Her curiosity whetted, she crosses the hall, ostensibly to feed the cat.

Before she goes, Bill comments on how tired she looks. Then growing impatient at her delay in returning, he follows, but the door is locked. His call brings her out after a while, and he notices at once the change. She no longer looks tired. He notes the color high in her cheeks, her girlishness, her sexual response to his kisses, the white lint on her back, suggesting a masturbatory occasion that parallels his own activity in the apartment.

Her echo of his earlier thoughts, "Maybe they won't come back" (*Where*, 70), suggests how far removed from reality they have become. It also speaks to the depth of their feeling that they have been deprived of a full life. Arlene is so swept away by this thought that it is a moment before she remembers she did not feed the cat or water the plants because she was distracted by some interesting pictures she found and wants to share with Bill.

Turning back, she discovers she has locked the key inside. This small event disturbs them beyond all reason, underscoring what was suggested by the unrealistic notion that the Stones might not return. It does not occur to them that they can get another key or call in a locksmith, for they have left the commonplace world of locksmiths and entered the enchanted world of the imagination.

Bill and Arlene Miller's behavior is familiar to readers of Carver's fiction, for the young narrator of "Nobody Said Anything" snoops, steals cigarettes, and masturbates. He also lies and, like Bill Miller, pretends to be sick in order to stay home and carry out his inquiries into the lives of others. Such transgressions are manifestations of the boy's desire to break the bonds of his life and enter into some liberating knowledge. They signal similar yearnings in Bill and Arlene Miller.

The positive aspect of "Fat" was one character's identification with another, the discovery of herself in the other, while her great disappointment was the inability to share her experience with Rita or Rudy or anyone else. Carver inverts that pattern in "Neighbors" by creating two characters who share the enchantment of imagination and for a brief period are able to break with their confining world. But only briefly, for at the close of the story, they are once again locked out of that other world, with no recourse but to return to their old unfulfilled life, which originated in the feeling that they alone among their circle of friends had somehow been passed over.

That emotion remained suppressed as long as they possessed the opportunity to enter the other world, but in the smallest of events—locking a key inside an apartment—the prospect of their old life returns as if blown in on an ill wind: "Her lips were parted, and her breathing was hard, expectant. He opened his arms and she moved into them. . . . They stayed there. They held each other. They leaned into the door as if against a wind, and braced themselves" (*Where*, 70).

The scene of these two individuals standing outside the locked door represents the story's essential emotion of perceived deprivation. That nothing tangible changed under the circumstances of taking care of an apartment is unimportant as long as one understands the significance of their subjective reality. Because they believed their life was unfulfilled, it was. As soon as they began to believe they were experiencing that fuller, more exciting life of the Stones, their life became exciting and meaningful. Emotionally primed, they are susceptible to any symbolic gesture. Thus, the event merges with the subjective state in the objective correlative of the locked door, releasing their dread from its unconscious suppression. The objective correlative helps to explain their unusual emotional response.

"They're Not Your Husband"

Discovering the other in oneself or discovering oneself in the other is an experience that broadens the individual's vision of self and the world. Taking on secondhand values without examining them, how-

17

ever, is constricting and lacking in imagination. In the first act, one heightens the sensibilities. In the second, the sensibilities are dulled, vision and awareness narrowed.

Earl Ober, an unemployed salesman in "They're Not Your Husband," takes the second course. All of his values come to him second-hand from the intervening agency of strangers. As he sits at the counter of the coffee shop where his wife works, two customers come in and take seats next to him. They note Doreen's figure and make a few snide remarks, including, "But some jokers like their quim fat" (*Where*, 33). Not wanting to be one of the jokers, Ober acts as if he does not know her when she offers him milk or coffee: "He didn't say anything. He shook his head when she kept standing there" (*Where*, 34). A moment later, he leaves his food to bolt for the door: "He heard her call his name, but he kept going" (*Where*, 34).

At home after leaving the coffee shop, Earl goes to bed, thinks about what has happened, and falls asleep. The next morning he announces that she needs to lose weight, not because it has ever bothered him before—"I never felt it was a problem before" (*Where*, 35)—or because of any concern for her health, but simply because he does not want to be one of the jokers. In order to persuade her to lose the weight, he brings the techniques of his profession (idle up to now) into play as he sells Doreen on the idea of a diet.

First, he makes her feel guilty about something she has never given any thought to: "I hate to say anything . . . but I think you better give a diet some thought. I mean it. I'm serious. I think you could lose a few pounds" (*Where*, 34). Then he backs off, as he might with a customer, attempting to disguise any eagerness on his part, pretending disinterest: "Maybe I'm all wet," "You're right, it won't be easy," "Okay, forget it" (*Where*, 35). Finally he closes the sell by suggesting she quit eating for a few days, implying that she can always go back to eating if it does not work out. This she agrees to try: "You've convinced me," to which he responds, "I'm a closer" (*Where*, 35).

He is a salesman. His wife defines him as such at the end of the story: "He's a salesman. He's my husband" (*Where*, 39). Soon, however, the image of the usurer exacting his pound of flesh replaces that of the salesman as the weight comes off, three and a half, five, nine and a half pounds. Each night, Earl Ober turns their home into a counting house, totaling Doreen's tips, smoothing out the bills, stacking the coins. Each morning, he counts her lost pounds on the scale he has purchased for that purpose, enters the numbers in an account book, and totals them until, at last, Doreen's appearance produces concern at work. He responds by instructing her to ignore her coworkers: "They're not your husband" (*Where*, 37), he says, dismissing the concerns of others and Doreen's health at the same time.

Although he is her husband, he refuses to consider Doreen's interests and badgers her to stay away from food. She might as well be an object or a product. But, of course, a salesman needs a product to justify himself. In the final scene, Ober returns to the coffee shop to see how his product is received by the customers. That reception, if successful, is supposed to establish that he is no joker.

He sits beside a man who glances at Doreen as she walks away, and Earl waits for some comment. When it does not come, he makes his pitch: "What do you think of that? . . . Don't you think that's something special?" (*Where*, 38). He has reduced her to a *that*, to a *something*, and a few lines beyond, to an *it*. Dehumanizing Doreen, he manages to make a disagreeable spectacle of himself, so much of a spectacle that the other waitress approaches Doreen and asks, "Who is this joker, anyway?" (*Where*, 39).

His behavior has identified him as a member of the group he most wants to avoid—jokers—and even here, the definition is secondhand, coming not from himself, but from another person. Perhaps being unemployed makes him defensive about what others think of him. Certainly he does not wish to have it confirmed in judgments about his wife. However, what he never learns is that people are truly defined, not by those they are with or by the objects they possess, but by what they do.

In his writing, Carver makes use of food in many ways—for example, as a substitute for sexual activity and as an emblem of sexual appetite. Here, though, he gives a different function to food. The more Earl Ober bullies his wife, depriving her of food, the more clearly we see him as a miser. When he comes in from a job interview and finds her eating, he calls her a slob, telling her to go on and eat, a tactic that has its desired effect. She returns to the diet, and Ober is pleased to see Doreen get paler and thinner until, at the end of the story, we see him publicly identified as the sort of person he least wants to be.

The qualities of this story are to be found in the voice, the dialogue, and the revelation of character. What gives pause, however, is the question of the author's attitude toward his characters. The development of Ober's character fails to provide the reader with any reason to care about him. There is nothing tragic or pathetic about him, nothing compelling. He is simply unpleasant, a foolish man who seems never to realize his shallowness or the harm he does. Neither the character nor the reader learns much that will help to reinterpret the world or expand one's vision. Ober is a type and as such he gives the story a satirical quality. Even so, there can be no question about the quality of the story's composition. It is well crafted and gratifying to the reader who wants to see Ober's cruelty and folly punished.

"The Idea"

"The Idea" is a brief story of double voyeurism that is closer to satirical caricature than "They're Not Your Husband." In it, the narrator waits inside her darkened room, anticipating her neighbor's appearance outside his own bedroom window, where he will watch his wife undress. She and her husband, Vern, have been observing the ritual every other night or so for three months, and it produces in them great appetites for junk food. On the night of the story, they watch, then eat. As the narrator cleans up, she discovers ants going into and out of the garbage can. She sprays them, washes her hands, and finds Vern asleep in front of the television, its picture rolling. Vern can sleep, but the narrator is so full of rancor about what she has seen that she can think of nothing but the ants. Soon she imagines ants throughout the house and turns on all of the lights. Looking out at her neighbor's house, she equates him and his wife with trash: " 'That trash,' I said. 'The Idea!' "⁹ Swearing, she sprays everywhere, spraying in a frenzy of extermination and sanitation even though no ants remain.

The puritan is still with us if H. L. Mencken is correct in asserting that puritanism is the gnawing suspicion that someone, somewhere, is having a good time. *Gnawing* is the operative word. The libidinal fixations of such puritans give them no peace. Unable to free themselves from their unhealthy preoccupations, they turn their rancorous energies toward the object of their revulsion; yearning for the obliteration of the other, they act out gestures of annihilation.

The narrator of "The Idea" is just such a puritan. She and her husband, Vern, live empty lives. Television is unsatisfying. Chain smoking defines Vern's existence. Stimulated by watching the neighbor's unusual ritual, Vern and the narrator have appetites only for junk food, which neither celebrates nor sustains human life. No wonder voyeurism has become the highlight of their evenings. A life reduced to watching television, smoking, and eating junk food is a fertile seedbed for hatred. In it, a gnawing rancor grows in place of charity and tolerance, pushing the character in this case toward vicarious and symbolic gestures of retribution.

Note, for example, the patterns Carver develops. From no evident source, discovered three months before, a trashy sort of behavior invades the neighborhood, and one can be certain, according to the narrator, of this invasion on dark and rainy nights. She is quite specific about these features, even emphasizing the point: "I've seen him out there when it's been raining too. In fact, if it *is* raining, you can bet on seeing him" (*Will*, 16).

Her reaction to the parallel action of ants suddenly invading her home from no evident source except a dark and humid place "somewhere beneath the pipes under the sink" (*Will*, 19) is consistent with her attitude toward the neighbor. She can do little about him—not that she actually wants to do anything that would deprive her of those prurient vigils—but she is able to transfer her unbridled rancor to the ants. Unfortunately, that is not the end of the matter. The ants have replaced the neighbor in her mind. Just as she wanted to share her discovery of the neighbor's behavior with Vern, she now wants to tell him about the ants and, no doubt, about her attack on them. Vern, however, is asleep, and the ants, although gone, are still in her thoughts.

It is a dilemma for the narrator, the source of her unrecognized despair. Without the object of her rancor, she might have to confront her empty life, and yet, that object generates a loathing that finds little outlet. So the narrator attempts to purge herself by killing ants and uttering expletives too vile to repeat.

Ultimately, what we have in "The Idea," as in "Fat," is the individual perspective as the primary element of significance. Unlike the narrator of "Fat," though, this one possesses no special insight into her own character, no identification with another—even though the parallels of voyeurism are inescapable—perhaps because her voyeurism and the neighbor's produce opposite passions, attraction in the one, revulsion in the other. Firmly sanctimonious in her condemnation, she never discovers herself in the other or the other in herself, and her character is such that she would deny the similarities if they were ever brought to her attention.

With such oppositions as attraction and revulsion, insight and blindness, we find two characteristic situations in Carver's work. Linking them is Carver's vision of alienation, which informs the narrators' shared isolation. Even when the individual in "Fat" has an insight, she finds it impossible to share that knowledge with another or she discovers in it the recognition of her own isolation.

"The Student's Wife"

The recognition of her own isolation is also the painful case in "The Student's Wife," a prefiguration of the indirect, minimalist fiction that unifies Carver's second commercially published collection of short fiction, *What We Talk about When We Talk about Love*. Drawn to Hemingway's notion that, once the writer knows that a fact, an aspect, or a condition is present, it can be removed from the fiction without losing the sense of its presence, Carver found an agreeable technique in the practice of stripping the story to its barest elements. Hemingway's comparison for this truncated genre was the iceberg, with its smaller mass visible above the water while the greater mass remained hidden, but felt, beneath the surface of the water. For Carver, this process was one that matched his own constrictive nature, and it later became the defining feature of *What We Talk about When We Talk about Love*.

In "The Student's Wife" (from *Will You Please Be Quiet, Please?*), the focus is on Nan who, dozing as Mike reads to her, dreams of caravans and walled cities, wakes suddenly when he stops, and wants something to eat. She tells him that the dream she was having, altered by the time she wakes, was about a lake and an older couple and their motorboat, which reminds her of a trip on the Tilton River when she and Mike were happy fishing and when he read to her from the *Rubaiyat*.

By now, however, Mike is sleepy. She wants him to rub her legs, to talk, to stay awake with her because she cannot go back to sleep. She lists what she likes and urges him to tell her what he likes, but he falls asleep, leaving her to face the night awake and alone. The experience affects her strangely, driving her into a state of unreasoning despair that is difficult for all but the insomniac to understand. For some individuals, insomnia can be the most serious problem of their lives. Failing to experience the sense of rebirth that comes with sleep, they feel all existence is continuous and occurs while others sleep. Unable to sleep, the sufferer feels out of control. For some, the sense of helplessness is so intense that any control, even determining the moment of one's death, would be a relief. Consequently suicide becomes a temptation.

Readers of Hemingway's "A Way You'll Never Be" will remember another insomniac, Nick Adams, who does not want to lose his way to Fornaci. Remembering the way to Fornaci is Nick's idea of staying in control. For Nick, as for many in real life, feeling out of control is a source of despair, and despair initiates the pull toward death, which presents itself as a solution to the problem.

As dawn breaks after her night of insomnia, Nan returns to the bedroom and sees Mike looking desperate in his sleep, his jaws clenched, and the sheets appearing grotesque in their whiteness. Both conditions are her interpretation and signal her emotional response to the sheets and Mike's sleep, each suggesting to her a shroud and Mike's death. At that point, she falls to her knees and prays: " 'God,' she said. 'God, will you help us, God?' she said" (*Where*, 32).

Having just passed the night awake and in a state of hysteria, Nan may have experienced an intuition of life without Mike. If so, Carver leaves it unexpressed. Nevertheless, the reader can see that Nan is unprepared for life without her husband if she is unprepared to pass even a single night alone.

For all its truncation and understatement—or perhaps because of it—the story has the power to convey to the reader Nan's undefined fear during her insomnia. Her fear differs from the emotional experience one finds in, say, a horror film; it recreates an encounter with the void that many feel at crucial points in their lives. The sudden knowledge that one, even in the presence of another, must face the void alone is a terrifying recognition, and no less terrifying if it comes as a vague apprehension.

In "Fat," the narrator attempts unsuccessfully to communicate her connection with the other. In "The Idea," the narrator, another insomniac, fails to see her connection with the other. In "The Student's Wife," however, the character comes face-to-face with her own otherness as an isolated individual alone with the unknown. Faced with such indefinable terror, she can only pray. Even then Carver leaves the reader with the feeling that this prayer is a futile attempt to make the leap of faith to the belief that God will help.

"Why, Honey?"

Nan's hysteria derives from her confrontation with the void, but Carver's unnamed letter writer in "Why, Honey?" has tangible reasons for her hysteria. She has received a query about her son, not an unusual event for mothers—except that this mother has changed her name and address specifically to get away from her son, who is now a powerful politician. The letter, characterizing her son as a pathological liar and a psychopath of unbounded cruelty, heightens her fear that anyone should have her name or address, especially anyone connected with or interested in her son.

A neighbor once saw him putting firecrackers into a cat's orifices. A friend revealed his salary was $28 a week instead of the $80 he told his mother. He lied needlessly about going on a school trip, and she found a bloody shirt in the trunk of his car after he purchased a gun and a knife and stayed out all one night. The day after one of his outbursts, she confronts him, asking why he lies needlessly about everything. His reaction is to drive her to her room, where out of fear she locks herself in.

After that, he leaves to join the U. S. Marines, serves his tour of duty, goes to college, marries, and enters politics. When he achieves fame and power, she becomes frightened, moves, changes her name, and gets an unlisted number. Nevertheless, she knows a powerful man could find her if he wanted to. She notices strange men in cars watching her and receives telephone calls with no one at the other end of the line. Now she has received a letter and wants to know how that person got her new name and address. The letter to her unnamed correspondent ends with a plea for an explanation.

Like "The Student's Wife," "Why, Honey" focuses on hysterical characters and has a truncated plot. The story provides an excellent example of Carver's shift from the Joycean stories of "Pastoral" and "Will You Please Be Quiet, Please?" to stories based on the unseen, but felt patterns of Hemingway's fiction, as seen, for example, in Hemingway's "Out of Season." We can see this principle of omission at work in the last paragraph of the story: "I also wanted to ask how you got my name and knew where to write, I have been praying no one knew. But you did. Why did you? Please tell me why?" (*Where*, 95).

Carver conveys his narrator's confusion and terror by disrupting her phrases and word choice and endowing her words with subsurface values. The first sentence is the only fully expressed complex structure in the paragraph, and the parts of its compound subordinate clauses are yoked by "how," the proper question word for this construction. The following independent clause is both a part of the first sentence (inadequately separated from it by the comma) and truncated in that it does not complete the thought "my name and . . . where to write." However, it is perfectly idiomatic and clearly understood.

The breakdown comes in the series of three elliptical expressions that close the letter. "But you did" depends on "knew," which precedes it, and it makes sense. Because "Why did you?" also needs a verb to complete the thought, it seeks the nearest one—"know"—and ambiguity follows. It is unidiomatic to say "Why did you know?" In her fear, the letter writer is concerned about motives. That concern is revealed by her switch from *how* to *why*. This confusion, along with her repetitions, creates the effect of hysterical insistence and a childlike simplicity. The repetitions, moreover, underscore her verbal limitations, giving the impression she is compelled to repeat herself because she lacks an adequate vocabulary to make herself clear, and the childlike question "Why did you [know]?" reinforces this impression of simplicity.

Finally, the juxtaposition of her childlike nature and what she has revealed about her son convinces us of her vulnerability, justifies her terror, and transfers to us some of the same emotion. Carver devises a character-revealing strategy when he has the mother place "Why did you?" so that the antecedent *know* suggests itself as the complement of her question.

"Are You a Doctor?"

The condition of alienation is said to be a twentieth-century affliction because it becomes pervasive during this period. It is seen in all areas of human activity to a degree that makes it one of the characteristic features of the age, and it is seen in many guises—the individual afraid to leave the house, the suspicious individual, the lonely individual whose condition may go unacknowledged until some occurrence forces the recognition.

"Are You a Doctor?" addresses the thematic variation of isolation as reflected in loneliness. The protagonist, Arnold Breit, is a careful man whose life is unremarkable. However, something extraordinary happens to him, and he is changed by it. That something is an errant telephone call from a woman he does not know. Clara Holt calls at the hour Breit expects to hear from his wife, who is out of town. She engages him in a conversation, compliments him, asks him to meet her, then hangs up. After the expected call from his wife, Breit answers the telephone when it rings again. It is Clara, this time saying that it is important that they meet.

The next afternoon, she calls again, imploring him to come to her apartment. He goes, learns from the little girl who answers the door that Clara is out, and starts to leave just as she returns. She gives the child some medicine and sends her off to her room while the adults sit at the table. When Breit learns that Clara's claim of mysterious urgency was expressed impulsively, he says he must leave, but rising to leave, he too acts impulsively and kisses her.

Back home later that night when the telephone rings, he answers it in a strange way, as if expecting Clara to be on the phone, but it is his wife. She says she has been trying to reach him since nine, remarks on his way of answering the telephone, and brings the story to a close by saying, "Are you there, Arnold? . . . You don't sound like yourself" (*Will*, 38).

In a telling sentence Carver sketches the conflict between the opposing forces of caution and loneliness: "He knew he should hang up now, but it was good to hear a voice, even his own, in the quiet room" (*Will*, 30). On principle, the careful man does not want strangers to have his unlisted telephone number: "He hadn't meant to be curt, but one couldn't take chances" (*Will*, 29). In such a conflict, the emotion with the greatest force will triumph, and loneliness possesses the power to subvert even the strongest habits of a lifetime. During the course of the first call and those that follow, Breit's characteristic caution is suppressed.

But not without some lingering precautions. After Clara calls again the next afternoon and implores him to see her, he continues to feel that he must be careful. Even after he yields to the temptation to go, he has the driver pass the address before letting him off, and while visiting Clara, he seats himself with special care: "He did not take the chair she indicated, but instead one that let him face the balcony, the hallway, and small living room" (*Will*, 36). Ironically, these precautions occur as he is making his rendezvous, his customary caution having already changed to such an extent that he comments on three separate occasions, "It's quite out of the ordinary, I assure you" (*Will*, 36), "It's unusual. . . . Quite unusual" (*Will*, 37), and "strange" (*Will*, 38).

Clara Holt reads in Breit's hesitation signs of his willingness to talk. Although she cannot know that he sits down while talking to her, she can read the meaning behind the fact that he is still on the line. She can also recognize his eager response to her compliment. The most telling sign, however, must be his request that she hold on while he goes for a cigar. His words upon returning to the phone are "I thought you might have hung up" (*Will*, 31).

These are the words of a man who wants some contact with another person, and they are enough to fire Clara's boldness as she asks, "Do you think we could meet somewhere we could talk? Just for a few minutes?" (*Will*, 31). Unlike Earl Ober, who was concerned about his wife's figure because of what others thought, these two are reaching out to each other without any regard for physical appearances, for she is "a small, pale, freckled woman" (*Will*, 35), with pale green eyes surrounded by dark circles. He claims to be old, a claim substantiated by his concern about his heart as he climbs the stairs of her apartment building. On the telephone and later in Clara's apartment, each recognizes a shared need in the other. Old or plain, each shows gratitude toward the other. He awkwardly kisses her when she stands. She raises his hand to her lips, saying, "You mustn't forget me, Arnold" (*Will*, 38).

The call, the visit, the kiss have altered him to such an extent that his words upon answering the ringing telephone, "Arnold. Arnold Breit speaking" (*Will*, 38), elicit from his wife the facetious, "Out living it up, Arnold?" (*Will*, 38). When he remains silent, she asks if he is there, noting that he does not sound like himself. There is an anticipation to his voice she has not heard before, and its source is the experience with Clara Holt. The need for human contact has overcome his customary caution and is now evident in his voice.

"Will You Please Be Quiet, Please?"

Just as the calls, the visit, and the kiss have altered Breit, so too does Ralph Wyman's discovery of Marian's infidelity in "Will You Please Be Quiet, Please?" alter him and his habitual, flawed belief that he knows his wife and understands himself. When this story was selected for *The Best American Short Stories* (1967), it brought Carver his first national recognition. Like his other award-winning stories, "A Small, Good Thing" and "Cathedral," it possesses a fully developed plot, a feature worth noting in a writer whose fiction up to that time is marked by truncation. It is also the longest story of his apprentice period.

Ralph Wyman is an ordinary young man whose father always insisted that life, although serious, is rewarding for those with purpose and strength. Wyman passes through the stages of joining a fraternity, drinking heavily, dabbling in literature and philosophy, and believing he is on the verge of discovering something significant about himself without ever testing the truth of his father's assertion. Like most people, he is attracted more to the fruits of lucrative professions than to their discipline.

Carver creates a directionless character guided externally by custom and habit. Coming under the influence of the persuasive Dr. Maxwell, Wyman reduces his drinking, bears down on his studies, becomes constructively active, meets Marian Ross, engages in a solemn, restrained courtship, and marries upon completing the requirements for a teaching degree. Measured by ordinary standards, he progresses as well as can be expected, passing from rudderless immaturity to acceptance of responsibility as husband, parent, and provider.

His values are decent and ordinary, as illustrated by his repugnance at Mexico's squalor and the open lust he believes he sees there on a trip with Marian. Thoroughly American, he yearns for the security of his native land on this trip, and by the time of the story's action, habit has dulled his senses, lulled him into thinking he understands Marian perfectly and himself as well. Wyman has measured himself without discovering anything significant. The emphatic point is that until the night Marian reveals her infidelity he manages to suppress his imagination.

He has had his opportunities to see Marian's nature—in Mexico when he observes her above on a balcony as someone apart from him and when he takes it into his head she has sexually betrayed him—but neither moment is realized. In fact, only Marian's impulsive query forces the issue. She wonders if he ever thinks about the night she went out with a friend to buy some liquor for their party.

Noticing her embarrassed expression, he denies thinking about it, then presses the matter until she discloses her infidelity and brings her sensuality sharply into focus. He had sensed its dangerous presence in her on that balcony in Mexico, but he refuses to face it (his own lack of passion makes it unimaginable) until her admission. Then the acknowledgment is wrenched gallingly from him: "But you've always been that way, Marian!" (*Will*, 233). The outburst underscores his past failure to admit her potential for passion. It also emphasizes the force of his present recognition.

That recognition causes him to partake of her experience vicariously, yielding to those unthinkable particularities that had previously tantalized him, but which he had suppressed. He suffers emotional intensities outside his own experience, conjuring from his imagination, which is unfettered for the first time, such intimate details as the unfastening of her garter belt and the chuffing *Go! Go! Go!* of her unleashed passion. Squalid, primitive Mexico had been for him the correlative of dangerous, open lust; and now, as if fleeing a foreign country, he rushes from the source of this intolerable reality and out into the night.

The reality goes with him though, for the epiphanous moment has said more about him and his lack of passion than it has said about Marian. "His mind filled with a swarm of accusations. . . . He looked down at his hands and noticed they had the same lifeless feeling they had when he had seen her on the balcony" (*Will*, 233). His feverish consciousness at the extreme limit of its intensity will allow no rest. All of his faculties are alert and defensive. His imagination, dormant for so long, invests otherwise innocent sounds and objects with the power to accuse: traffic horns proclaim his cuckoldry; a rack of antlers confronts him with the deception. His measurement of himself is displaced by suffering, and for the first time in his life, Ralph Wyman is alive.

His odyssey takes him drunkenly to an oyster house bar and the men's room to confront his image in a mirror, knowing his life has suddenly changed, wondering if others can pinpoint such a momentous event and change in their lives. It is significant that the cataclysmic event is his discovery of Marian's infidelity, not the event itself. His change dates from this moment. Joining a card game, he observes the other players and wonders if they have ever been deceived.

Later, he wanders into a liquor store and buys a half pint of rum, its tropical label no doubt reminding him of Mexico and the clerk's "Got you a little something tonight?" (*Will*, 245) reinforcing that reminder. His trek through the bar district ends when he is roughed up by two citizens of the night and left on the pavement. At dawn, he turns homeward.

By the time Wyman gets home, he has indeed come a long way. At the beginning of the evening, he was sure he understood himself and what he could do; by the time he arrives home the next morning, he understands only that certain things have been done, but he has no idea what to do about them now or tomorrow or any other day. However, in his misery and confusion, he finds life and its changes astonishing.

Love and jealousy have revealed over the course of the night that neither is a continuous single passion, but rather an infinity of successive loves and jealousies. At the end of "Will You Please Be Quiet, Please?" Ralph Wyman is different from the person who began the night insensibly grading papers, absolutely sure of himself and his relations with Marian. The crisis resolves itself finally to his amazement and with his apparent acceptance of the old Marian and the new Ralph Wyman, for the old one died somewhere in the night.

The First Phase

It is convenient to call the period that produced the fiction of *Will You Please Be Quiet, Please?* an apprenticeship. Carver was not widely known then. His work rarely appeared in well-paying periodicals (although *Esquire* and *Harper's Bazaar* did publish his fiction). But the quality of his early writing has withstood the passage of time, careful scrutiny, and sober judgment remarkably well. Indeed, as so often happens with the work of our best writers, that early fiction has grown in stature.

It would be misleading to suggest that Carver was completely un-recognized. The fiction that has been dealt with here was nominated for the National Book Award in 1977, and as has been pointed out, "Will You Please Be Quiet, Please?" was anthologized in *The Best American Short Stories*. Nevertheless, his second collection of stories, *Furious Seasons*, was published by the small publisher Capra Press, and the next commercially published collection of fiction did not come out until 1981, during which period he remained one of America's well-kept secrets except for readers who followed serious fiction in the quarterlies. Not until Knopf brought out *What We Talk about When We Talk about Love* (1981) did Carver receive the sort of attention that would admit him to the pages of *The Atlantic* and *The New Yorker.*

The motifs of alienation and encountering the other, often in the guise of the grotesque, continue in the second phase of Carver's writing, as do the stories about fishing and hunting, which played significant roles in his emotional life. What distinguishes the two periods is his method; in his second phase he begins the great experiment of radically reducing every fiction to produce the minimalist standard. The structure changes, but the voice and the concerns remain the same.

Breakthrough: *What We Talk about When We Talk about Love*

When *What We Talk about When We Talk about Love* appeared in 1981, its spare style and unity of method caught the attention of reviewers and readers alike. Suddenly Raymond Carver, working consistently in a minimalist idiom, had people talking about the renaissance of the short story and about his new collection as the masterpiece of minimalism. After he had labored for almost two decades in relative obscurity, its impact created a breakthrough for him and opened up new opportunities. His sudden fame also left him with a feeling of wonder and elevated confidence: "It's a continual amazement to me, this attention that's come along. But I can tell you that after the reception for *What We Talk About*, I felt a confidence that I've never felt before" (Simpson, 210).

The handsome little volume with the long catchy title provided something else as well, a selection of previously published stories subjected to rigorous cutting, "cutting everything down to the marrow, not just to the bone" (Simpson, 204). Of the eight stories in *Furious Seasons* (1977), half were pared down and republished in *What We Talk about When We Talk about Love*. By comparing stories from *Furious Seasons* with the later versions of *What We Talk About* we can discover insights into Carver's method of composition, attitudes, and goals during this period of rigorous cutting.

The technique of severe cutting, which Carver admittedly took to its extreme, was not new. Hemingway perfected it to produce the elliptical stories college students study in introduction to literature classes. In *A Moveable Feast*, he chronicled the discovery of what would become one of his most persistent strategies—the effect of limited fictional visualization: "It was a very simple story called 'Out of Season' and I had omitted the real end of it which was that the old man hanged himself. This was omitted on my new theory that you could omit anything if you knew that you omitted and the omitted part would strengthen the story and make people feel something more than they understood."[10]

31

His new theory came to be known as the iceberg principle because of the similar disproportion between the visible and the unseen, but felt, parts of his stories and that of a floating mass of ice. A less poetic, but more accurate, image might have been the ghost limb of amputees—once there, now missing, but still felt. However, biographer Carlos Baker correctly notes that the truncation of the seminal "Out of Season" was not Hemingway's foremost aesthetic discovery. The significant revelation was his new narrative technique of "developing two intrinsically related truths simultaneously, as a good poet does with a metaphor that really works."[11]

Because truncation announces itself, while "the metaphorical confluence of emotional atmospheres" (Baker, 109) loses itself in the flow of narrative, truncation is what caught the critics' attention in Raymond Carver's second commercial collection of fiction and earned the author his celebrity status as America's premiere minimalist writer. While attention to a minimalist idiom is proper and necessary, it behooves us to look beneath the obvious to see how the idiom works.

One method Carver uses to develop character and theme is the juxtaposition of two or more characters exhibiting opposing traits, creating a situation in which the exemplary behavior of a subordinate character forms an implicit critique of the other. Another is a technique that emphasizes the convergence of "emotional atmospheres" linking characters in the story. Such a convergence occurs when comparable features appear in two or more characters.

This situation is especially effective if it consists of the main and a subordinate character. It is easier, first, to view the subordinate without the distracting complications normally invested in the main character; second, to see his or her traits in isolation, as happens in "Sacks," the first story I will discuss in this section, when the reader observes the hysterical behavior of a minor character dancing to the music of the jukebox; and then, third, to note the confluence of their separate emotions in their similar behavior. The result is a clarifying resonance—that is, in "Sacks," the mutual amplification of two discourses: the father's tale of infidelity and the narrator's punctuating notice of and comments about the hysterical woman during his father's story.

Implicit in this critique is the notion that a detailed occurrence in a narrative can be correlated with other elements, which function as metaphorical antecedents or as explanatory appositives verifying the principle of finding meaning in narrative patterns. The source of this intuitive conviction is the long tradition of Western literature, which insists on a recoverable meaning. Every detail is pertinent and arranged to point the reader toward that meaning. Under this assumption, any private symbolism or element that does not contribute to the whole is considered a flaw or at best irrelevant.

Some measure of the direction Carver was taking during his phase of intense constriction reveals itself in a comparison of "Sacks" from *What We Talk About* and an earlier version of the story, titled "The Fling," published in *Furious Seasons*. Examined together the two versions announce Carver's determination to free his fiction from even a hint of bulk.

"Sacks" ("The Fling")

The narrator in "The Fling" meets his father at an airport, accepts a sack of sweets for his wife and children, and joins his father for drinks in the airport lounge. While listening to his father's story of adultery, he observes a woman at the bar flanked by two attentive men. His father's story is punctuated by this woman's behavior, which culminates in a frenetic dance to the music of the jukebox.

According to the father he was alone when Sally Wain delivered a sack of Stanley Products for his wife. He let Sally in and their conversation developed into a sexual encounter. The encounter became an affair. One night Sally's husband, a truck driver, came home unexpectedly, and the father made his escape by leaping through the picture window. The betrayed husband took a room in a hotel, where he committed suicide by stabbing himself. At the end of the father's tale, it is time for his son to catch a plane home, and he leaves without the sack of gifts for his wife and children.

In "Sacks" Carver reduces the space given to the hysterical behavior that links the dancing woman to the emotional abyss of the father by cutting almost two pages of her dance—as if the parallels are too glaring in the earlier version. Although the narrator never mentions the connection between this woman's hysteria and his father's behavior in his affair with Sally Wain or indicates in even an inarticulate manner that he recognizes the link, his attention is focused on the woman while she is at the bar and during her dance, and the resonance of the event is such that the reader can sense her frenzy as an implied metaphor of the father's adultery.

Carver also deletes the following sentence: "Yet something else tells me he was beyond help, beyond anything I could do for him, and that the only thing that transpired between us in those few hours was that he caused me—*forced* might be the better word—to peer into my own abyss."[12] We can see this deletion as an example of Carver's distrust of articulate characters and an example of his desire to excise themes, leaving behind only the characters' obsessions.

Recognition and articulation of emotional kinship now excised, the connection must reveal itself by means of metaphorical implication, juxtaposition, and such innuendo as occurs in the veiled comment that ends the story:

> On the way to Chicago, I remembered how I'd left his sack of gifts on the bar. Just as well. Mary didn't need candy. Almond Roca or anything else.
> That was last year. She needs it now even less.[13]

The husband who forgets gifts for his wife does not have her as the focus of his attention or affection, and such comments as those cited above speak volumes about his lack of feelings for her, implying that their marriage is now out of season too.

In changing the title from "The Fling" to "Sacks," Carver emphasizes the recurring image that marks beginnings and endings in this narrative. The father greets his son with a sack of sweets. Sally Wain's arrival at the door with a sack of Stanley products for the narrator's mother initiates the domestic transgression and leads to the breakup of the narrator's parents' marriage. The narrator forgets to take his father's sack of gifts with him, and when he remembers it later, he makes the oblique remark about his wife just quoted, which closes the story and reveals the emotional abyss of his marriage.

On the verge of revealing the truck driver's death in "Sacks," the father stops and leaves it unreported. In light of Hemingway's revelation that he cut Peduzzi's suicide from the end of "Out of Season," it is unlikely Carver's cutting of the truck driver's suicide is simply fortuitous, but in neither instance is the death the most important feature. Both stories are improved by the omission of unnecessary elements. However, it is—in the words of Carlos Baker—"the metaphorical confluence of emotional atmospheres" that provides meaning for the attentive reader, as well as bearing tacit witness to Carver's admiration for Hemingway's method.

Interestingly, in discussions of their work, both writers emphasize their cutting while failing to mention the important aesthetic device of investing parallel figures with intrinsically related truths, and yet, the latter technique is essential to the minimalist idiom. Reduced scales benefit from multiple implications suggesting density, a process in which the human mind is an accomplice, for the way the world is structured, the mind and the senses try to infer meaning from elliptical signals that require some effort to interpret. Such signals are a result of natural and technical limitations. The eye blinks, omitting some of the visible. The camera shutter blinks, omitting much of what occurs. Yet we piece our fragmented world and movies together in apparently seamless motion.

When reading elliptical fiction, we have to interpret events from incomplete accounts stitched together with the thread of assumptions we bring to the task. By means of these assumptions, we are able to experience the insight, even though the narrator is not. Carver has limited the character's understanding (expressed in the early version: "caused me—*forced* might be the better word—to peer into my own abyss"), an authorial act that confirms his acknowledged distrust of insights: "They don't help any. They just make things harder" (*Fires*, 24).

The structure of "Sacks" is the same as that of "Fat" except that Carver reverses the point of view. His narrator in "Fat" relates her experience to Rita, who fails to understand what she has just heard: "'That's a funny story,' Rita says, but I can see she doesn't know what to make of it" (*Will*, 6). In "Sacks," the narrator assumes Rita's role as the listener who, by asking if Sally Wain is still in Redding, reveals he has missed the point of his father's story. His father's response is one of incredulity: "'You don't know anything, do you?' my father said. 'You don't know anything at all. You don't know anything except how to sell books'" (*What*, 45). And yet, a strong intuition makes itself felt, a nagging impression that the narrator is in the same emotional state as his father, but unlike the father is still denying his condition at the end of their meeting.

"The Third Thing That Killed My Father Off" ("Dummy")

The radical reduction of scale characterizing *What We Talk about When We Talk about Love* does not alter Carver's recognizable voice. He retains, for example, the highly stylized repetitions, distinctive syntax, and diction familiar to readers of *Will You Please Be Quiet, Please?* We still find his penchant for deformed anatomies as manifest in the grotesque other, the recurring obsessive personality, and the pervasive despair. What he breaks with are the Joycean epiphanies, the derivative imagery of "Pastoral" and "Will You Please Be Quiet, Please?" and the relatively fleshed out story lines (never very pronounced in any case, except for "So Much Water So Close to Home," until later phases of his writing).

Indeed, Dummy in "The Third Thing That Killed My Father Off" is a prime example of Carver's obsessive, grotesque other who, like the obese customer of "Fat," affects the lives of other characters: "He was a little wrinkled man, bald-headed, short but very powerful in the arms and legs. If he grinned, which was seldom, his lips folded back over brown, broken teeth. It gave him a crafty expression. His watery eyes stayed fastened on your mouth when you were talking—and if you weren't, they'd go to someplace queer on your body" (*What*, 90). In details like the compacted limbs, grotesquely folding lips, and broken teeth, Carver foreshadows the violent conclusion of the story by evoking a sense of pent-up force waiting to explode.

Mute, deaf or at least poor of hearing, and isolated in a marriage to an unfaithful wife, Dummy is a laborer at a sawmill in Yakima. The narrator's father works there also, as a saw-filer. While most of the men at work tease Dummy, the narrator's father does not. There is an unspoken bond between them. He, for example, suggests that Dummy send off for bass fingerlings to stock his ponds, and Dummy orders them.

After he acquires the fish, a bizarre change comes upon him. As his wife grows bolder in her infidelities, he becomes estranged from the workers and emotionally attached to the bass. When they are large enough to provide sport, the narrator's father pressures Dummy to let father and son thin out the fish, arguing reasonably that it will help the fish. At first reluctant, then obstinate, he becomes irrational in his refusal, and this attachment to the bass brings about a rift in the relationship between the two men. Later, a flood carries away the fish. Pushed to the edge, Dummy kills his wife and himself, and the experience marks the final decline of the narrator's father.

The original version of the story, "Dummy," contains several telling statements that help in an interpretation: "I believe it somehow marked the end of the halcyon period of his life, too, for it wasn't much later that his own health began to fail," and "For me, Dummy's death signalled the end of my extraordinarily long childhood, sending me forth, ready or not, into the world of men—where defeat and death are more in the natural order of things" (*Seasons*, 9). At the end of the story, we read, "But it seemed to me life became more difficult for him after that, that [father] was never able to act happy and carefree any more. . . . Like some kind of mysterious and terrible signal, it seemed to herald the misfortune that dogged our family in the coming years" (*Seasons*, 26).

Carver cuts these comments and severely restricts the narrator's explanatory remarks in "The Third Thing That Killed My Father Off." He also reduces the portrait of Dummy to a few fundamental traits—handicapped, innocent, capable of strong emotional attachment, and coarsely wronged by an unsympathetic spouse—traits designed to render the least articulate character while also evoking compassion.

Putting his faith in the fish, Dummy could feel protected from any betrayal. Carver's characters often attempt small goals to support their lives, but as he put it, "people don't succeed at what they try to do, at the things they want most to do, the large or small things that support life" (Simpson, 201). In his simplicity, Dummy has not reckoned on nature, which had cheated him already by depriving him of speech.

The rains come and then the flood, breaking into the ponds and taking away the fish. His repressed sense of outrage, like the flood waters, finally bursts its boundaries, manifesting itself in murder and suicide. The events, characterization, and imagery evoke compassion and pathos in this portrait of isolated, inarticulate humanity, and those emotional qualities provide its strength.

The portrait also represents the extreme of reducing the human figure to the condition of inarticulate, befuddled victim. In a final grotesque image identifying Dummy with the black bass, Carver brings the story to a close: "After a time, an arm came out of the water. It looked like the hooks had gotten Dummy in the side. The arm went back down and then it came out again, along with a bundle of something. . . . That arm coming up and going back down in the water, it was like so long to good times and hello to bad" (*What*, 103). Death by water, death and water, it is an image readers have grown used to in literature and in the symbolism of baptism, but there is no rebirth in this story.

"So Much Water So Close to Home"

Along with death and rebirth, water is associated with madness, chaos, and destruction; in "So Much Water So Close to Home," water possesses chaotic, destructive power. Awful discoveries are borne on its currents. Terrible visions are seen in its depths. The version of the story that appears in *What We Talk about When We Talk about Love* contracts its space to such an extent that a different fictional syntax is created. Published in three different forms, in its first and in its final publications, it is twice the length of this sharply reduced version. The vocabulary is notably austere; sentences, paragraphs, and sections are markedly briefer than those in the longer versions of the story, where both paragraphs and sections are combined to create denser pages and sentences have many more qualifiers. Without the intervening analysis of the longer versions, scenes shift closer to each other, and the pacing of the narrative is altered, becoming sharper, more abrupt, the dislocations much more jagged.

"Fat" was Carver's prototype for the kind of story wherein two characters have access to the same event, by means of one character relating the event to the other. In both "Fat" and "Sacks," the one who hears about the event fails to grasp the full implications of what he or she hears. However, in "So Much Water So Close to Home," after learning that her husband, Stuart, and his friends have found the body of Susan Miller, Claire Kane allows her imagination, in this variation on the form, to identify with the victimized other.

Stuart and his friends, instead of sending one of the men back to report their find when they come upon the nude body, proceed with their fishing expedition, cutting the trip short by only a day. Stuart never acknowledges the barbarity of their behavior or his responsibility in the course of events. Realizing the morning after his return that Stuart has made love to her while keeping the discovery from her, Claire reacts emotionally, as if his behavior were a violation of her.

Becoming more and more unhinged, she recalls the murder and decapitation of Arlene Hubly, a girl in her high school. The drift of her memory toward that old event coincides with her own sense of disembodiment, for she sees her reflection in the water and begins to imagine herself dead, floating face down, eyes open, carried along by the breeze, separated from her body.

An authenticity resides in Carver's presentation that we readily accept. So it is not surprising to have the experience confirmed by modern science. According to Oliver Sacks, in *The Man Who Mistook His Wife for a Hat,* when deep disturbances of body perception or image exist, "such depersonalization or derealization must always occur."[14] It does occur in Claire, for she loses her "sense of proprioception, the fundamental, organic mooring of identity" (Sacks, 50) when she discovers what has happened on the fishing trip.

Yet, even at this intense moment of transference, she realizes that "nothing will be any different. We will go on and on and on and on. We will go on even now, as if nothing had happened" (*Where*, 166). Feeling this acutely, she slaps Stuart, even as she thinks, "We need to help one another. This is crazy" (*Where*, 166). It is an informing scene and an important recognition on her part, but both scene and realization are cut from the version in *What We Talk about When We Talk about Love*.

As soon as the body is identified and funeral arrangements made, she drives to the young woman's town and attends the ceremony. In the radically cut middle version, the trip seems to be cathartic. Upon her return she lets Stuart unbutton her blouse and urges him to hurry before their son, Dean, comes in. This closure does indeed indicate that nothing has changed or will. However, the version in *Where I'm Calling From* closes with a physical demonstration of Stuart's violence and with Claire's accusation, "For God's sake, Stuart, she was only a child" (*Where*, 177); in this version, there can be no reconciliation between Stuart and Claire.

One way of looking at this story might be to view it as another of Carver's treatments of obsession. A neurotic woman with a history of emotional problems is unexpectedly linked with a murder victim through her husband's chance encounter, thus triggering a memory of the forgotten Arlene Hubly, murdered and decapitated by the Maddox brothers, who like Stuart maintained their innocence. What makes this a much more interesting work of fiction, though, is Claire's imaginative response.

Stuart is made miserable by the consequences of the event, but it produces no lasting effect on his inner life. He has been part of an event without recognizing its full implications, while Claire is radically changed. He is concerned only about the disturbed relationship with his wife, while she recognizes the parallels between the men's behavior and the rape itself, which is allowed, even encouraged, by society's equation of women with objects.

Claire's imagination operates in her derealization of herself and in her experiencing the scene as the victim, sensing the violence to another as if it were committed against her: "I look at the creek. I float toward the pond, eyes open, face down, staring at the rocks and moss on the creek bottom until I am carried into the lake where I am pushed by the breeze" (*Where*, 166). She has intuited that a violation of Susan Miller or Arlene Hubly is a violation of all women.

Explicit evidence for such a reading is found in both the first and last published versions of the story. Claire determines that "two things are certain: 1) people no longer care what happens to other people; and 2) nothing makes any real difference any longer" (*Where*, 167). She goes on to articulate her recognition that something significant has happened without permanent effect: "Yet nothing will change for Stuart and me. Really change, I mean" (*Where*, 167). This conclusion is confirmed by Carver's closure in the cut version, for in that rendition her complicity with Stuart's sexual advances can be seen as yielding to his dominance and attempting to reconstruct on an unstable basis a world that has been reduced to chaos.

In the final version, however, she alters the relationship, refusing to have anything sexual to do with Stuart, whose gestures, looks, and actions justify her fear of violence from him: "He catches my wrist before I can strike again and raises his own hand. I crouch, waiting, and see something come into his eyes and then dart away" (*Where*, 166). Referring to herself in the third person, she recalls that "once, during a particularly bad argument, over what she can't remember, five years or so after they were married, he tells her that someday this affair (his words: 'this affair') will end in violence" (*Where*, 168).

The last sections of the longer versions reinforce the theme of violence when he attempts to take her by force: "And then I am lifted up and then falling. I sit on the floor looking up at him and my neck hurts and my skirt is over my knees" (*Where*, 176). Finally at the end, he demonstrates that she is at his mercy: "Last night, around midnight, Stuart breaks the lock on my door. He does it just to show me that he can, I suppose" (*Where*, 177). Her act of imagination has made life with Stuart, life as it was, impossible. Their responses to the event have revealed how little they have in common, and she does in fact make certain, by refusing to yield to him, that something will change.

Maintaining the overriding method of paring in *What We Talk about When We Talk about Love*, Carver cuts the above important passages. As a companion piece for the other stories in the collection, the reduced version complements the book in this form. Such cuts notwithstanding, by the time Carver came to the task of preparing his final selection of fiction, he returned to the ending of the longer story, revealing his later thoughts on the two versions and his final preference.

That ending may seem the more pessimistic and less appealing of the two, but it is not. Of course there is always the attraction of reestablishing the original equilibrium, but if that happens, she returns to her former life. Then she is right that nothing ever changes. By closing with the accusation, "For God's sake, Stuart, she was only a child," Carver makes a return to the old life impossible. Like Nora Helmer in Ibsen's *A Doll's House,* Claire Kane cannot return to her life as a mere domestic object.

Claire's emotional chaos recalls a number of Carver's stories in which the lives of the characters unravel until, at last, all that remains is disequilibrium. As one of the distinguishing features of the Carveresque, this slide toward disorganization warrants discussion. For centuries, chaos was viewed as exceptional in Newton's clockwork universe; biological structures, determined by initial conditions, evolved toward greater and greater complexity; and trajectories moved toward their ineluctable ends. If disequilibrium occurred, forces worked for a return to equilibrium. And so it was with literature: a literary work began in a state of equilibrium, was disrupted by crisis and complication, and had to be brought back to equilibrium by a resolution of the conflict.

Although there is a temptation to view Carver as heir to the naturalists, he often breaks with a determinism in which initial conditions shape the outcome. Up to a point, his work follows the classical pattern of equilibrium and perturbation, but it can and often does deviate from the traditional return to equilibrium. One way of swerving from the conventional outcome is to introduce a random attractor, in this case Arlene Hubly, who disrupts the trajectory of the characters and causes their initial conditions to be forgotten until it is too late. By then, the memory of early hopes and expectations is just a memory and no longer part of an active plan.

"Gazebo"

Such is the case with "Gazebo," a story that concludes in tumult, the lives of the main characters devastated. Duane and Holly have sequestered themselves in one of the upstairs suites of the motel they manage, ostensibly to talk out their domestic problem. Because they have formed the habit of making all their important decisions while drinking, they have provided themselves with a bottle of whisky and are on a binge, with the motel office locked, the telephones unanswered, the customers ignored. Holly is on the verge of a breakdown. Duane has hit emotional bottom. Although they had hopes for a peaceful and happy life as they grew older, Duane's infidelity with the motel maid has disturbed the trajectory of those hopes.

They drink, they frolic sexually, they sleep, and Holly tries to jump from the upstairs window. But the domestic problem remains, and the customers beat on the door downstairs and blow their car horns while inside the locked office the telephone rings. Duane and Holly have reached the end of something. Whatever follows they will have entered a new life. This much Duane realizes as Holly recounts an anecdote from their past.

They had stopped at a farm outside of Yakima, Washington, for water. The elderly couple who owned the old house asked them in and shared a cake with them before showing them a gazebo out back under some trees, where a long time before, people gathered on Sundays and listened to men playing music. Holly says she had thought they would be in a similar situation when they were old: "Dignified. And in a place. And people would come to our door" (*Where*, 109).

From their vantage point in the suite, Duane can look out over the parking lot at the customers knocking on the door below. The sad irony is that Holly has seen the future, but with a cruel twist. She had meant a place of their own, but they are in place owned by strangers and serving strangers, a place in which they have become strangers to themselves. People come to their door for lodging, but they are in no shape to accommodate them, and, much more important, these people are not friends congregating at their place for communal sharing and goodwill.

A fitting place for musical gatherings and fellowship, the gazebo evokes an image of a beautiful view, the literal meaning of the synonymous *belvedere*. There is speculation, as well, that *gazebo* is a formation of *gaze* and the Latin ending for the future tense *-ebo*. Holly's gaze beheld a beautiful future. The reality, however, is sordid, reduced to chaos, without center, as Holly confesses, "I've lost control" (*Where*, 104), but the characters are not bad people. They are decentered, pathetic, no longer—in their fevered and dulled states—even pretending to revel in living.

Something decent has died in them. They have lost their connections to each other, a loss that reveals itself in their entropic turning away from the other and in their excess of frenetic, unused energy as manifest in their sexual desperation and her attempted suicide: "That morning she pours Teacher's over my belly and licks it off. That afternoon she tries to jump out the window" (*Where*, 104).

It might be easy to see this story as a condemnation of infidelity and life wasted by drink, but that would be too easy. The tone of the story suggests that the inevitable course of life is not to blame for this couple's fall from grace (they must accept that responsibility), but the tone, which is neutral, neither judgmental nor apologetic, does indicate that a spontaneous inexplicable change is responsible for the destruction of the bond between them.

Although, as Sacks reminds us about drunkenness, "these states can 'release' memory, and all of them can lead to a re-experience and reenactment of the past" (Sacks, 145), the drinking and the infidelity seem more symptomatic than causal, ineffectual ways of handling this loss of connection. The story serves to remind us of the continuous becoming that confronts all people. Some handle it better than others. Some, like Duane and Holly, fail utterly and are left with only an incontinent nostalgia that accentuates the pain. Holly's remembrance of the gazebo is a recurring instance of the impotence and hopelessness found in yearning for the past and its lost or imagined equilibrium.

Time after time, we encounter some sort of fibrillation in Carver's work, a character whose spasms signal an emotional loss of control and the chaos of his or her life. Typically this reaction is triggered by the slightest event whose importance is magnified beyond what one would expect, and typically its occurrence signals the fiction's closure.

"Why Don't You Dance?"

On rare occasions, Carver initiates a story that takes place after the storm. "Why Don't You Dance?" is one example of fiction initiated in the aftermath of such a tempest, a domestic storm that is inferable from the detritus (household objects for sale in the front yard) and an oblique comment made by the man as he dances in his driveway with the girl: "'That's right,' the man said. 'They thought they'd seen everything over here. But they haven't seen this, have they?' he said" (*Where*, 120). The effect of coming upon the ruins directs the reader's attention to the characters who encounter this destruction and must either make something of it or fail to interpret it.

An omniscient narrative, "Why Don't You Dance" possesses angles of vision that fluctuate between an unnamed, middle-aged man and the young couple, also unnamed, wanting a few items to furnish their apartment. Having moved everything out of his home for a yard sale, the man returns from a trip to the store with alcoholic beverages just as the young man approaches the front door to see if anyone is home. As the characters come together, the process of bargaining begins, although right away it ceases to be a moment of negotiation and becomes instead one of those intervals of abandonment so often associated with emotional devastation:

> "I was thinking fifty dollars for the bed," the man said.
> "Would you take forty?" the girl asked.
> "I'll take forty," the man said. (*Where*, 118)

The pattern is repeated for the television set—stated price, an offer at $10 below the suggestion, acceptance—until even this semblance of negotiation breaks down after the man offers them a drink, directing their attention to glasses wrapped in newspapers and packed away in a carton. When the young woman, deciding she wants the man's desk, asks how much he will take for it, he dismisses the question with a wave. " 'Name a figure,' he said" (*Where*, 119).

He puts on a few old records and encourages the couple to dance in his yard. They do, once, twice, until the young man, feeling the effects of his drinks, has had enough of dancing. Then the young woman asks the man to dance, receives him with open arms, pushes her face into his shoulder, pulls him close, and says, "You must be desperate or something" (*Where*, 121).

Weeks later she is still talking about the experience in order to discover its meaning. When she finally ceases to speak of it, we are surely justified in believing that she has failed to discover the implications of what she has encountered.

In this brief story, only five pages in *Where I'm Calling From*, we again discover Carver's debt to Hemingway and his extension of the iceberg principle. We are not told the man has reached bottom, that he is married or divorced; yet we can see from all the signs that he is estranged, a drunk, no longer motivated by the circumstances that made a household. He is still with the house. The furniture is his responsibility. Clearly someone has left him. This is the future Duane and Holly could see in "Gazebo." It is also a potential future for the boy and girl of this story.

By having the girl refer to the middle-aged man as an old guy, by showing the girl's ignorance of the song titles, and by revealing her derision of the records, thus underscoring the absence of any shared experience, Carver emphasizes the generational gap even more than the facts of the situation dictate.

By juxtaposing one couple's beginning and the aftermath of a dissolution, Carver creates a tension that is immediately felt in the reading. He brings the girl to the threshold of understanding that dreams gone sour often manifest themselves in desperate acts and that this desperate man must have been in love when he was her age and starting out in a relation like hers. Carver even has her attempt to reach across that threshold of understanding by talking about the experience as if its meaning would suddenly break through if only she repeats the story enough times. "She kept talking. She told everyone. There was more to it, and she was trying to get it talked out. After a time, she quit trying" (*Where,* 121).

As so often happens in Carver's stories the character remains uninstructed, almost, but not quite, grasping the significance of an event he or she has experienced. Typically the character will have a physical manifestation, reacting hysterically or losing his motor function, knowing that something has gone drastically wrong, but without realizing precisely what it is.

The story contains one of those epiphanies of imperceptiveness, caught adroitly in the expression, "After a time, she quit trying," that suddenly reveals the essence of the character's condition and what she has to look forward to. From a disinterested vantage, the reader must see the patterns Carver has constructed and cross that threshold to understanding from which the character is barred.

In "Why Don't You Dance?" we can see back into the man's chaotic past without the aid of details and ahead into a similar chaotic future, not of the man, but of the young couple. Human experience almost dictates it. Their responses will be different when the crash comes, but the motivating factors will be familiar. It is as though this desperate man is looking into the future and saying, "Why don't you dance? Enjoy it, for one day you won't," but the point Carver is making is not the man's realization. He does not see into the future either. It is the girl's imperceptiveness.

"What We Talk about When We Talk about Love"

Readers often complain that nothing happens in stories like "What We Talk about When We Talk about Love." Two couples in this story— Mel and Terri McGinnis and Nick and Laura—sit around a table, drinking gin and talking about love. Several varieties of emotion, existing under the single rubric of love, enter into the conversation either in passing or at length—spiritual love, carnal love, chivalric love, idealized devotion, and even the sort of complex torment that exhibits itself in abuse, often murder, and sometimes suicide. Mel the cardiologist does most of the talking, and much of that about Terri's former lover, Ed, who abused her, threatened murder, and finally succeeded on his second attempt at suicide.

Mel's other anecdote focuses on an elderly couple injured in a car wreck. The injured husband drifts into depression because the bandages prevent his seeing his wife while they are in the hospital.

That is it—ostensibly. But of course that is not all there is to the story. The little ironies and revelations of the story help to develop a complete narrative that no summary can ever sufficiently provide. Although not explicit, they are capable of revealing the inability of these characters to see themselves or each other honestly.

The most graphic scene is Terri's anecdote: Ed beat her one night, dragging her around the room by her ankles, repeating, "I love you, I love you, you bitch" (*Where*, 128). She says Ed loved her so much he tried to kill her. Terri's interpretation of such evident ambivalence agrees with Ed's—it is love. That an individual deems his life not worth living without her must seem to her the highest testimony of her value. That Ed might have killed himself as one last attempt to punish her or that he might have taken his life as an act of self-loathing is unacceptable to Terri. That interpretation would devalue her.

Up to a point it is advantageous for Mel to see more clearly than Terri. If he sees that Ed's passion hardly qualifies as love, he need not feel quite as emotionally threatened by the dead lover, but only up to a point. It would not, for example, enhance Mel's self-image for him to see the parallel between Ed's violence toward Terri and his violent feelings toward his former wife. "She's allergic to bees. . . . I'm praying she'll get herself stung to death by a swarm of fucking bees" (*Where*, 139). Then again a moment later, "Sometimes I think I'll go up there dressed like a beekeeper. You know, that hat that's like a helmet with the plate that comes down over your face, the big gloves, and the padded coat? I'll knock on the door and let loose a hive of bees in the house" (*Where*, 139). Nor does Nick, the narrator of the story, his girlfriend, or Terri seem to notice the parallel pattern. It remains invisible to all but the reader.

At the same time, Mel may sense his own susceptibility to sentimentality (in his desire to be a knight), immediate gratification (in eating, drinking, and getting high), and compulsiveness, features of arrested emotional development shared with Ed, for he says about himself, "I like food. . . . If I had to do it all over again, I'd be a chef, you know?" (*Where*, 135). Mel's alcoholism and attraction to pills also testify to this self-gratifying impulse. Spiritual love, the idealized state of chivalric love, and the devotion of the elderly couple, having made a strong impression on him, may represent antidotes to or, at least, havens from his emotional immaturity. Or, as is more likely, extensions of that immaturity, for such imaginary escapes are further proof of underdevelopment.

He characterizes the years he spent in the seminary as the most important years of his life, yet he left that life. He maintains that had he the opportunity to come back in a different life, he would come back as a knight, an impossible, sentimental wish. Moreover, he idealizes the elderly couple's love when he asserts that their example "ought to make us feel ashamed when we talk like we know what we're talking about when we talk above love" (*Where*, 134). This idealized state amazes Mel, who says, "I mean, it was killing the old fart just because he couldn't *look* at the fucking woman" (*Where*, 138).

Nothing happens. Four people sit around a table talking about love. Or so it seems, but the term needs defining. Distinct, sometimes opposite states are experienced under the name of love: spiritual devotion, sexual attraction, fellowship, emotional dependence, and more. From Mel's incredulity, the reader can rightly infer that nothing he has ever felt as love could be favorably compared with what he found in the elderly man who was depressed because he couldn't see his wife. Whatever these characters sitting around the table drinking gin speak of when they talk about love, it is different from what he has seen in the hospital.

Different enough for him to realize that their talk around the table and elsewhere never approaches the real thing, and yet Mel remains partly blind to the truths of love and self. Not so the careful reader, for a while at least, because Carver dramatically juxtaposes varieties of experience that, when seen together, sharpen their lines of difference and no longer pass unquestioned for love. In life though, just as in literature, moments of the most vivid clarity soon fade, leaving us to fall back on signs and symbols to guide us in love or in life.

Maturity: *Cathedral*

If a great number of critics hailed the publication of *What We Talk about When We Talk about Love* in 1981 as the establishing event of Carver's career, it is the arrival of *Cathedral* three years later that confirms his place among short-story writers of the first rank. The confirmation results in part, however, not from a continuation of what established him, but from his manifest growth and the more generous spirit visible in his work.

The defining features of Carver's fiction alter during the period between the two books. The voice remains the same, but the vision becomes less grounded in despair. The fictional framework is enlarged and reinforced by traditional structures. Empty spaces fill with beginnings, middles, ends. Truncations vanish; where once the narrative halted in emotional tumult, the story continues and equilibrium is restored. Despair becomes redemption; the alienated are reconciled. Hardboiled realism turns out to be allegory with a soft center.

The techniques, situations, and effects of popular forms become the tools, material, and goals of his fiction. He exploits the melodrama of what was once the exclusive province of daytime television (now also under primetime lights and cameras), the thrills of detective fiction, and the convictions of a culture's assimilated lessons.

It is a sign of Carver's maturity that he makes these adjustments skillfully, with a power and quiet confidence seldom seen in the toilers of such genres. The sureness of a writer at ease with himself is felt in his willingness to develop complete narratives that shun the old poetics of withholding, in his willingness to permit affirmative resolutions, and in his opening up of the narrative to include aspects (sentimentality, for example) traditionally dismissed by literary critics as unsuitable for serious fiction.

Aside from being exemplars of maturity in a fine craftsman who has enlarged his reach and grasp, certain stories in *Cathedral* provide excellent opportunities to note the retrieval of sentimentality and religious melodrama from the storehouse of cultural assumptions and the restoration of their aesthetic value during the 1980s. When literary historians look back, they will wonder what so modified tastes that melodrama could move from radio to the hot klieg lights of daytime television, from afternoon to primetime drama, and finally from the electronic medium to award-winning serious fiction. "But in a knowledge of authors and their times," as Paul Valéry observes, "a study of the succession of literary phenomena can only excite us to conjecture what may have happened in the minds of those who have done what is necessary to get themselves inscribed in the annals of the History of Letters":

> If they succeeded in doing so, it was through the concurrence of two conditions which may always be considered as independent: one is necessarily the production of the work itself, the other is the production of a certain *value* in the work by those who have known and liked it once it is produced, those who have enforced its reputation and assured its transmission, its conservation, its ulterior life.[15]

That value bestowed by others—editors who like and select a work for publication, critics who transmit its reputation, and members of grants and awards panels who determine material and symbolic stamps of value—was denied for most of the twentieth century, as Jane Tompkins has pointed out, to works that were accused of trading in "false stereotypes, dishing out weak-minded pap to nourish the prejudices of an ill-educated and underemployed female readership."[16] However, with the major institutional changes of the 1980s, a visible shift in literary criteria took place, and no story better illustrates this shift than "A Small, Good Thing."

"A Small, Good Thing"

"A Small, Good Thing" provides a clear contrast between the quintessential Carveresque, as represented by "The Bath" in *What We Talk about When We Talk about Love,* and the new fiction of *Cathedral.* Certain therapeutic themes highly charged with iconographic intensity make their appearance in the story, reinforcing convictions so deeply held that we are often unaware of their presence or force. Moreover, the story's record of awards and reprintings testifies to the cultural shift toward sentimentality that characterizes the decade of the eighties and expresses the degree to which devalued elements appreciated during this shift.

49

Unlike numerous stories by Carver in more than one version, "The Bath" and "A Small, Good Thing" are not variations of the same story, although the characters, initiating situation, and crisis remain the same. In the McCaffery-Gregory interview, Larry McCaffery identifies them as two versions of a story taking radically distinct courses. Carver amends his interviewer's definition, calling the narratives "two entirely different stories" that he found difficult to think of "as coming from the same source" (McCaffery, 66). On this point, the author can be trusted, for certain parallels between Vladimir Nabokov's "Signs and Symbols" and Carver's "The Bath" insist that the former exercised an influence on Carver as he composed the latter. To that extent "Signs and Symbols" was a source for the "The Bath," but not for "A Small, Good Thing."

In both omniscient narratives, parents of a hospitalized son spend his birthday worrying about his life in the care of medical people. In the Nabokov story, the son is grown, suffering from insanity, and in danger of killing himself in the asylum; in the Carver story, the son has been struck by a car, is in a coma, and in danger of dying from the trauma. In both stories three telephone calls function as menacing signs. The falling back on signs and symbols in "The Bath" underscores Carver's fondness for a sense of threat, which he confesses to in "On Writing": "I like it when there is some feeling of threat or sense of menace in short stories. I think a little menace is fine" (*Fires*, 17).

"The Bath" opens with Ann Weiss's visit to a baker and an order for a birthday cake. On Monday, the day of Scotty's birthday party, the boy is struck by a hit-and-run driver: "He fell on his side, his head in the gutter, his legs in the road moving as if he were climbing a wall" (*What*, 48). Here Scotty resembles Nabokov's image in "Signs and Symbols" of an unfledged bird knocked from its nest and twitching in a puddle.

Scotty picks himself up and returns home where, before slipping into a coma, he tells his mother what happened. At the hospital, the parents begin their vigil, watching for signs of recovery, dealing with medical people as they search for signs of the problem and taking turns going home for a bath. During the father's trip home the baker, without identifying himself, calls twice, making cryptic remarks about the cake that was not picked up. Disoriented in his fear for Scotty's life, the father does not make the connection or mention the calls to Ann upon his return to the hospital.

Finally persuaded to go home and freshen up, Ann encounters an African-American family waiting at the hospital for news about their son Nelson. A moment of mistaken identity and a disconnected exchange underscore the emotional states of the respective individuals. In the last brief scene, Ann reaches home, and the story closes with the third and final telephone call from the baker: " 'Scotty,' the voice said. 'It is about Scotty,' the voice said. 'It has to do with Scotty, yes' " (*What*, 56).

The effect of this closure is powerful in the context of Ann's emotional state, even to the reader who knows the caller is the baker. She is terrified. Her only child is in a coma at the hospital. She has just encountered another mother waiting for word about her hospitalized son. She has not slept for a long while and is disoriented. The last thing she needs to hear at this moment is the jarring ring of a telephone with a sinister voice from the other end of the line encouraging her worst fears with ambiguous words.

Unlike many of Carver's stories that end in overt loss of control, this one provides clear motivation for a breakdown. However, because Carver has made the provision this time, an actual breakdown becomes unnecessary, and he leaves it out. In the empty space following the last full stop, the reader involuntarily experiences the powerful emotions that Ann would feel. The result is a story that exemplifies the Carveresque as well as any story Carver ever wrote.

And yet, he rewrote "The Bath" as "A Small, Good Thing," expanding it to three times its original length, giving it a fully developed structure with a beginning, middle, and end, and a resolution of reconciliation, effectively removing both the Nabokovian influences and its distinctly Carveresque qualities, while at the same time creating for it a much wider appeal than his stories usually enjoy.

As a truncated, indirect work of fiction, "The Bath" remains consistent with the other stories of *What We Talk about When We Talk about Love*. Along with the title story of the collection, "So Much Water So Close to Home," and "Why Don't You Dance?" it is one of the most memorable fictions in the book, but the synergetic force of the whole collection is what makes itself felt among those readers and critics who respond favorably to the work.

Readers without patience to seek out the hidden complexities of indirect or elliptical narration tend to reject Carver's fiction on grounds that the stories are incomplete. They fail to find a sense of development or proper closure. Accustomed to overt conflict and its clear resolution, they believe the stories are devoid of significance, of events that would explain the characters' motivation and retarded emotional states, and of consequences when explanatory events do occur, as in "The Bath." Even when taken together as a coherent mosaic of scaled-down narratives, the stories portray unpleasant realities without relief. All too often, these readers complain, Carver chooses to eliminate character-shaping relations and to give only the result of the character's static confusion.

Such objections ought not to be dismissed without consideration, yet a little reflection reveals that they fail to take into account the method of indirection, which has become the technique of choice in this century. This method, in conjunction with Carver's desire to focus on a limited time or action for the sake of realism, has contributed to his minimalist reputation, a designation that irritated him. It also helps to form what I call his defining signature. Granted, the technique derives in part from an obsessive desire to avoid great glares and had evolved in Carver by the time of this collection to the point that even the epiphany—which might have created a sense of closure, dynamism, and meaning—had been trimmed of all devices that would render its meaning immediately clear. And yet, the patterns of Carver's fiction—repetition, parallelism, opposition, shared elements—have the power to reveal missing scenes, relations, explanations, the past, and the future. The lesson of these truncated narratives is that much of their merit can be found in the omitted parts, which patience and care can flesh out.

However, no such claim can be made about "A Small, Good Thing," for neither its structure nor its theme owes anything to truncation or the signs and symbols of Nabokovian menace. Instead, it depends on sentimentality and a different category of characterization, on cultural myth and a therapeutics of passion for its effect.

Howard and Ann Weiss, their child Scotty, and the unregenerate baker appear in both stories, but compare the two Howards:

> It had been a good life till now. There had been work, fatherhood, family. The man had been lucky and happy. (*What*, 49)

> Until now, his life had gone smoothly and to his satisfaction—college, marriage, another year of college for the advanced degree

in business, a junior partnership in an investment firm. Fatherhood. He was happy and, so far, lucky—he knew that. (*Where*, 282)

College, an MBA, a junior partnership in an investment firm. This Howard is like no previous character in Carver's fiction, and the family doctor is a stereotype that viewers of soap opera will recognize immediately: "The doctor was a handsome, big-shouldered man with a tanned face. He wore a three-piece blue suit, a striped tie, and ivory cuff links. His gray hair was combed along the sides of his head, and he looked as if he had just come from a concert" (*Where*, 284–85). The only stock items missing are the overcoat and silk scarf these doctors are usually wearing when they come from the symphony to take pulses and lift eyelids. There is, furthermore, the melodramatic scene of Ann and Howard performing their vigil while Scotty lies in a coma:

> "I've been praying," she said.
> He nodded.
> She said, "I almost thought I'd forgotten how, but it came back to me. All I had to do was close my eyes and say, 'Please God, help us—help Scotty,' and then the rest was easy. The words were right there. Maybe if you prayed, too," she said to him.
> "I've already prayed," he said. "I prayed this afternoon—yesterday afternoon, I mean—after you called, while I was driving to the hospital. I've been praying," he said.
> "That's good," she said. For the first time, she felt they were together in it, this trouble. She realized with a start that, until now, it had only been happening to her and to Scotty. She hadn't let Howard into it, though he was there and needed all along. She felt glad to be his wife. (*Where*, 286)

Whether Scotty will live in "The Bath" is an open matter—he is alive when the story ends with the baker's telephone call underscoring the menace—but he must die in "A Small, Good Thing" in order to fulfill the thematic requirements of sacrifice and redemption. As Tompkins argues, "Stories like the death of little Eva [in *Uncle Tom's Cabin*] are compelling for the same reason that the story of Christ's death is compelling" (Tompkins, 127). The pure die to redeem the unregenerate, and through Scotty's death, the baker will be brought back into the world, where people know how to behave.

In *Madness and Civilization*, Michel Foucault notes the moral tenor of water treatments and travel for disturbed behavior and emphasizes the correlation between salvation and a return to the world: "If it is true that the techniques of immersion always concealed the ethical, almost religious memories of ablution, of a second birth, in these cures by movement we can also recognize a symmetrical moral theme, but one that is the converse of the first: to return to the world, to entrust oneself to its wisdom by returning to one's place in the general order of things, thus forgetting madness."[17]

Along with a therapeutics of movement and immersion, Foucault devotes attention to beliefs in cures by passion: "By subjecting the nervous fibers to a stronger tension, anger gives them more vigor, thus restoring their lost elasticity and permitting fear to disappear" (Foucault, 181). Foucault's emphasis on the necessity of the immediate, on cures by passion, and on cures by regulation of movement wonderfully parallel the conceits of Hemingway's anachronistic hunter in "The Short Happy Life of Francis Macomber." Here are the white hunter Wilson's explanations of Macomber's newfound courage: "Hadn't had time to be afraid with the buff. That and being angry too. Motor car too. Motor cars made it familiar. Be a damn fire eater now. He'd seen it in the war work the same way. More of a change than any loss of virginity. Fear gone like an operation. Something else grew in its place. Main thing a man had. Made him into a man. Women knew it too. No bloody fear."[18] It is Macomber's need to react without thinking, what Foucault calls the necessity of the immediate, that forestalls his fear. When he had time to think about the wounded lion earlier, he became frightened, and in Wilson's world, cowardice is a sign of disturbed behavior. Having been a car racer, Macomber's reaction in the moving car is nothing more than a familiar reaction brought on by the regulation of movement. And of course he is angry about his wife's infidelity— Foucault's cure by passion. Along with other eighteenth-century notions and cultural traces, a therapeutics of passion has leached down to us through the centuries and is still with us in the fiction of Hemingway and Carver.

Elaborating his morality play and perhaps taking his cue from Hemingway's example, Carver resorts to cures by passion, giving Ann Weiss an angry vigor as she realizes the telephone calls have come from the baker. She insists on their going to the shopping center. Confronting the man, "She clenched her fists. She stared at him fiercely. There was a deep burning inside her, an anger that made her feel larger than herself, larger than either of these men" (*Where*, 299). This correlation of Foucault's curative anger purifies Ann's condition, concentrating her thinking, fortifying her resolve, leaving her, as Wilson might say, with "no bloody fear."

For the baker's anger and consequent behavior, Carver administers a prescription of fear, curing his patient, according to Foucault, just as eighteenth-century doctors would have done: "Fear, in the eighteenth century, was regarded as one of the passions most advisable to arouse in madmen. It was considered the natural complement of the constraints imposed upon maniacs and lunatics" (Foucault, 180). Confronted by the infuriated Ann Weiss, the baker loses his bluster, which is replaced by a constraining fear. "A look crossed Ann's face that made the baker move back and say, 'No trouble, now'" (*Where*, 299).

A conversion follows. He confesses, repents, and asks forgiveness. Bread and coffee are brought out, and the three of them commune until dawn. A sense of redemption is everywhere felt in the atmosphere of this resolution. What we have here is religious allegory, for the iconography of this reconciliation belongs, not to the neorealist phase of Carver's earlier fiction, but to the tradition of typological narrative with its doctrine of theological types, what Tompkins calls "a narrative aimed at demonstrating that human history is a continual reenactment of the sacred drama of redemption" (Tompkins, 134).

The popularity of a work is certainly indicative of the values of its time, but not necessarily of literary values. In the twentieth century, at least, there has been a clear line between popular literature and serious literature. However, when popularity and critical opinion agree, the convergence speaks with authority about the aesthetics of the period, expressing something profound about the culture that produces such a convergence.

"A Small, Good Thing" was published in *Ploughshares*, honored in *Prize Stories 1983: The O. Henry Awards* and *The Pushcart Prize* (1983–84), and reprinted in the *Ploughshares Reader: New Fiction for the Eighties* (1985). And yet, there has been some dissent, noted by Carver when he told McCaffery and Gregory, "I've had people tell me they much prefer 'The Bath,' which is fine, but 'A Small, Good Thing' seems to me to be a better story" (McCaffery, 66).

If the author's judgment can withstand the passage of time, a radical shift in literary values must be seen to have occurred in the 1980s, a shift that may seem perplexing to future critics. However, Jane Tompkins, asserting the power of nineteenth-century sentimental narratives, may have located the source of that shift. In "A Small, Good Thing,"

Carver creates the illusion of realistic fiction, but, as Tompkins explains about *Uncle Tom's Cabin*, "what pass for realistic details . . . are in fact performing a rhetorical function dictated" by the story's ruling religious paradigm of sacrifice and redemption (Tompkins, 136).

A set of governing beliefs, organizing and sustaining a pervasive cultural myth, "invests the suffering and death of an innocent victim with just the kind of power that critics" have traditionally withheld from such literature (Tompkins, 130), but critics are not free-floating entities unaffected by powerful social currents. When a cultural shift occurs, they react to prevailing attitudes just as others do, adjusting literary criteria to meet cultural pressures. It may be that this need to adjust best explains the critical reception of "A Small, Good Thing." It may be that, at the deepest levels, even tough-minded critics are governed by our most persistent cultural myths.

"Vitamins"

Although evidence of the melodramatic stands demonstrably present in "A Small, Good Thing," the story is just one of several in *Cathedral* that rely on emotional effects and materials drawn from popular forms. The fictional situation of "Vitamins," which exploits the thrills of risky sex, personal danger, and racial fears found in much detective fiction, is another. It develops in the following manner: Patti sells vitamins door-to-door and supervises other women doing the same. The characters forming the core of the group—Patti, Sheila, Donna—are experiencing bad times. Vitamins aren't selling well, and their personal lives are falling apart. Sheila is the first to forsake the business, taking off for Portland when she finds Patti unresponsive to her advances: "One night this Sheila said to Patti that she loved her more than anything on earth. Patti told me these were her words. Patti had driven Sheila home and they were sitting in front of Sheila's place. . . . Then Sheila touched Patti's breast. Patti said she took Sheila's hand and held it. She said she told her she didn't swing that way" (*Where*, 184). Sheila's sexual advance is the first of three such events in the story, Patti's rebuff the first of three such rejections. Together, they shape the informing patterns of the story.

The second occurs at a Christmas party thrown by Patti to cheer up the group. Attached to Patti, but attracted to Donna and finding himself with her in the kitchen, the narrator embraces her, receives a warm response, but is told, "Don't. Not now" (*Where*, 186).

This refusal is clearly more deferral than rejection, a conclusion that is confirmed when Donna shows up later as the narrator is leaving the hospital, where he works nights on the cleaning crew. They begin their night together by going to an after-hours jazz bar owned and frequented by African-Americans. They are joined in their booth by Khaki, Benny, and Nelson, the latter just back from Vietnam with a human ear in his silver cigarette case and $500 in his wallet.

The central event of the story occurs in the booth. It is also in this crucial scene that we discover significant parallels with popular detective fiction. Indeed, we encounter specific parallels with a chapter from Timothy Harris's detective novel *Good Night and Good-bye* (1979).

Like Donna and Carver's narrator, Harris's detective, Thomas Kyd, finds himself in a bar booth threatened by hostile blacks. At one juncture, "Mojo's hand snaked out and grabbed my collar while the guy next to me leaned his weight against me and took hold of my ear. . . . 'He got two, Mojo. He don't need this ear. Let's take him in the back room and do an operation.'"[19] Then later, Mojo tells the detective, "You thought Baltimore was jiving you when he talk about cutting off your ear. The dude's bad, man. How many ears you cut in Nam, Baltimore?" (Harris, 149).

We might also compare two other passages, the first from Harris's novel: "I stood up, and this time Moth and Baltimore moved quickly to let me out of the booth. 'I haven't got the stomach for the work. I was in Nam. I've seen guys cut ears off stiffs. It never did anything for me except make me sick.' I smiled into Baltimore's watchful ill-humored face. 'That's strictly an animal act you got there, friend. That shit belongs in a cage'" (Harris, 150). And the second from Carver's story:

> He looked around the booth. He looked at Nelson's wallet on the table and at the open cigarette case next to the wallet. He saw the ear.
> "That a real ear?" Khaki said.
> Benny said, "It is. Show him that ear, Nelson. Nelson just stepped off the plane from Nam with this ear. This ear has traveled halfway around the world to be on this table tonight. Nelson, show him," Benny said.
> Nelson picked up the case and handed it to Khaki.
> Khaki examined the ear. He took up the chain and dangled the ear in front of his face. He looked at it. He let it swing back and

forth on the chain. "I heard about these dried-up ears and dicks and such."

"I took it off one of them gooks," Nelson said. "He couldn't hear nothing with it no more. I wanted me a keepsake." (*Where*, 194)

Carver's handling of the situation seems mythic in its use of a blind character (metaphorically blind in this instance) as intervening agent, clairvoyant in perceptions, oracular in pronouncements. Nelson looks at the couple with his alcohol-reddened eyes as if trying to place the narrator and sees that they are betraying Patti. "What I want to know is, do you know where your wife is? . . . while you setting [*sic*] here big as life with your good friend" (*Where*, 192). He suggests that Patti is also out with someone and makes the third sexual advance of the story, offering Donna $200 to perform fellatio on him.

Donna's rejection of this offer is the final refusal of the story, but like her protestation at the party, it is not sincere. She confesses to the narrator as they return to the hospital parking lot, having made their escape, that she needs the money and is sorry she did not accept the $200. Now, she too will leave for Portland. "I'm not going in. I'm leaving town. I take what happened back there as a sign" (*Where*, 195).

It takes a particular state of mind—as Isak Dinesen simply, but convincingly demonstrates in *Out of Africa*—to find a sign in an event. The state is brought on by a maelstrom of disasters. What seems at first a mere coincidence of circumstances becomes the dominant factor of one's life, evolves into an obsession, and eventually is seen as having a necessary central principle, which if only known could bring the chaos into a coherence that can be dealt with. In that final stage, the individual is prepared to find a sign in anything that lends itself to the situation.

For Dinesen it was the confrontation between a white cock and a chameleon. In an attempt to save himself, the chameleon opened his mouth and shot out his clublike tongue, which the cock plucked out. The gruesome event struck her profoundly and left her shaken. In her state of mind, it was irrefutable testimony to danger: "I looked down on the stones and dared not look up, such a dangerous place did the world seem to me."[20] Donna has also seen the cock pluck out the chameleon's tongue, so to speak, in her willingness to take money for sex, and she has taken it for a sign, which makes up her mind for her.

When the narrator reveals that he has also been thoroughly shaken by the event, we are left with but one conclusion. Although not admitting it, he has had a sign, as well, and the experience has altered him. He returns home and starts looking through the medicine cabinet, spilling pills in the sink, making a racket, and disturbing the fully dressed but sleeping Patti, who wakes and blames him for letting her oversleep.

It is true that the narrator reacts to Nelson's threats in a way similar to Mr. Harrold's reaction in "Pastoral" to having a gun on him, and were it not for the pattern of sexual advances and rejections in the story, suggesting human relations as the theme, we might suspect "Vitamins" of being a variation on the theme of mortality. However, there can be no dismissal of the pattern.

First, the narrator is *told* by Patti that Sheila made a pass and was gently rebuffed. Then he makes a pass at Donna and is put off. Finally, Nelson makes a pass at Donna. She refuses him while actually wanting to accept. Such a pattern strongly suggests that saying *no* is not final for these characters. In two out of three instances the narrator can be certain of that.

And what about Nelson? Is he an avenging angel or oracle? Whatever he is, the narrator cannot dismiss his words. His judgment must be reckoned with, for he takes one look at the couple and says to the narrator, "You with somebody else, ain't you? This beautiful woman, she ain't your wife. I know that" (*Where*, 192). Then he says that Patti is out with another man. He also reads Donna correctly. She would, admittedly, have taken the money for the sex.

And finally, he yells after the couple, "It ain't going to do no good! Whatever you do, it ain't going to help none!" (*Where*, 195). That too is true. Like a spirit, Nelson's presence seems to follow them. In three out of four instances, the narrator can be certain that Nelson's reading is accurate. Perhaps he is also accurate about the fourth. Perhaps Patti is with another person.

Badly shaken by his encounter with Nelson, the narrator cannot be certain of much, least of all that Patti has not betrayed him with Sheila or someone else. Like Wyman in "Will You Please Be Quiet, Please?" he may have failed to see Patti's potential for passion—or seen it and refused to acknowledge it. In either case, he must confront the possibility, and that makes him an altered person.

Recalling Carver's past use of the themes of mortality and human relations, we might be justified in asking if he is merely repeating himself or contributing something new to his old preoccupations. After a moment's thought, we can observe one difference immediately: the two themes, treated separately in earlier stories, are rendered complex in "Vitamins" by combining them in a narrative pattern that subordinates the mortality issue to the question of human relations, although the threat of death or harm is the catalyst that directs our attention to the characters' relations.

All of the events—the drinking, the sexual disruptions and disappointments, the futile attempts to escape their dismal plights by fleeing to Portland or Arizona, as Patti and the narrator speak of doing—underscore the narrator's recognition of what their lives have become: empty, meaningless, oppressed by poverty and the pressures of trying to make ends meet. As Patti says early in the story, "I don't have any relief. There's no relief!" (*Where*, 187), then later, "Middle of winter, people sick all over the state, people dying, and nobody thinks they need vitamins. I'm sick as hell myself" (*Where*, 188). And it's true. These characters are spiritually sick, beaten down by a life over which they have no control. Things are falling apart, and there are no vitamins that will help. In this condition, they are typical Carveresque characters confronting a depressing nihilism.

Typical they may be, but Nelson is another matter altogether. Like Scotty in "A Small, Good Thing," he possesses mythic qualities; Scotty is a Christ figure, and Nelson both the blind seer and avenging angel. Both are representations of the symbolic in someone real. Carver's essays "On Writing" and "Fires" offer helpful information about Nelson's function. The first essay underscores Carver's fondness for creating a feeling of threat, the "sense that something is imminent" (*Fires*, 17), that certain forces are relentlessly set in motion. The second essay reveals the origin of Nelson, who changes the direction of "Vitamins." In "Fires," Carver recounts how he was once interrupted by a telephone caller seeking someone named Nelson. Noting the inflections of black English in the caller's speech, Carver imagines his characters in a situation that demands the Nelson we encounter: threatening, the sole custodian of judgment and prophecy, perceiving the scene and foretelling the outcome, able to transcend everyday realism. Nelson is a character, in essence, much closer to Sophocles' Tiresias than to the powerless, inarticulate people we are accustomed to seeing in Carver's fiction.

Carver's exploitation of white America's fear of the black male and other persistent myths separates the fiction of *Cathedral* from earlier Carveresque fiction while, at the same time, linking it with detective and sentimental genres. Even when Carver returns to his old form, as he does in "The Bridle," capturing the colloquial diction and syntax of his narrator, there is something different about the work. It is fleshed out, no longer without resolution, and there is a felt sympathy, a pathos not always present in the early stories and almost always missing from stories in *What We Talk about When We Talk about Love.*

"The Bridle"

Sympathy emanates from Carver's enterprising narrator-apartment manager, Marge, who has installed a professional chair with sink and turned the front room of her living quarters into a beauty parlor, where she collects the rents, writes receipts and, most important, talks to interested parties. As up-to-date as any current member of the National Hairdressers and Cosmetologists Association, she disdains the title of *beautician* and calls herself a *stylist.*

In charge of a corporate-owned apartment complex in Arizona, Marge and her husband, Harley, observe the arrival of a family of four in flight from the chaos of their life in Minnesota. Marge rents them an apartment, but it is not until later, when she gets the new tenant into her beautician's chair and relaxed by a manicure, that Betty starts talking.

Back in Minnesota after his first wife left him, Holits met and married Betty. Their life together began well enough, but then something happened. Holits bought a horse, took to betting on it, and gambled away the farm. Although Carver does not include the scene in this story, one need not imagine what passed between the travelers before their departure; Carver provides the prototype in "Vitamins":

> Then we got to talking about how we'd be better off if we moved to Arizona, someplace like that.
> I fixed us another one. I looked out the window. Arizona wasn't a bad idea. (*Where,* 187)

The idea occurs, distilled in the alembic of a mind beholding nothing. The character contemplates the prospect of departure, its unfulfilled promise, and symbolic escape. It is a familiar scene in Carver's fiction, and Carver leaves it out in "The Bridle."

Now in Arizona, their possessions reduced to an old station wagon, clothes, and a bridle, they are hoping for a change of luck and a new life. However, once again, something happens. Under the influence of drink and at the urging of others, Holits attempts to leap from the roof of the pool cabana into the water, misses, splits his head open, and is left permanently addled. Before long, the family gives up the apartment and moves on, leaving the bridle behind.

No doubt Holits had retained the tackle to flatter himself about his knowledge of horses, but by the time it is overlooked or left intentionally, the harness, reins, and bit have come to be, not an instrument Holits uses to control and guide brute force, but rather the symbol of Holits's condition, controlled rather than controlling. As Marge puts it at the end of the story, "If you had to wear this thing between your teeth, I guess you'd catch on in a hurry. When you felt it pull, you'd know it was time. You'd know you were going somewhere."[21]

One feels the power of that image, a negative force that life exercises on individuals, especially those on whom Carver focuses his attention. More often than not, they are incapable of stating with any precision what they sense. Consequently, we must interpret their strange physical reactions or indirect comments that say important things in commonplace utterances.

Still under Marge's spell in the chair, Betty remembers that her school counselor once asked what her dreams were. It was a question without an answer then, but asked the same question now, she would reply, "Dreams, you know, are what you wake up from," adding to Marge, "You don't know what it's like" (*Cathedral*, 200).

But Marge knows. She is on the point of revealing just how clearly she knows when Carver deftly restrains her by guiding Harley into the room. She never finishes, but the reader sees the affinity between these two wives, sees as well the similarity between Holits and Harley. Betty's burden is Marge's too. As Marge expresses it, "Sometimes I lie awake, Harley sleeping like a grindstone beside me, and try to picture myself in Betty's shoes. I wonder what I'd do then" (*Cathedral*, 201). Her curiosity is rhetorical, for she must know that she would continue her life as it is, exchanging one stonelike husband who sees and understands nothing of the drama she is witnessing for another.

After the family leaves, Marge inspects the apartment and finds it clean: "The blinds are raised, the bed is stripped. The floor shines. 'Thanks,' I say out loud. Wherever she's going, I wish her luck. 'Good luck, Betty'" (*Cathedral*, 208). With this sympathetic farewell expressed across an unknown space, Marge once again acknowledges her affinity with Betty. She may not be able to articulate the significance of what she has experienced, but she can hardly fail to detect the presence of forces that control people against their will and damage them. She expresses as much by thinking of the bridle.

"Cathedral"

To weave sympathy, sentimentality, and melodrama into the fictional fabric of *Cathedral* with the assurance of an artist unburdened by lingering doubts and have the mature quality of the writing widely acclaimed by critics and readers alike—these are notable accomplishments perhaps best explained by the originality of the title story, which first appeared in *Atlantic Monthly* and was reprinted in *Best American Short Stories, 1982*. Carver's imaginative invention may find its explanation in something as simple as his use of the rarely seen opposite of an archetypal pattern.

"Cathedral," more than any other story, is the emblem of the new Carver. The disillusioned first-person narrator, often but not always a child, is one of literature's most familiar structures and a chief example of dynamic characterization. In the paradigm, the protagonist discovers a profound truth that is necessary in order to take one's place in mature society. The structure goes back as far as Oedipus, and individuals who have read Turgenev's "First Love," Joyce's "Araby," and Sherwood Anderson's "I Want to Know Why" will recognize this paradigm immediately. "Cathedral," however, provides the rare opposite of this familiar type: a narrator who discovers a life-affirming truth without the pain. While it is true that such a story runs a risk of sinking into the sentimentality of "A Small, Good Thing," Carver contrives to avoid the hazard in an instructive manner.

Robert, a blind friend of the narrator's wife, who comes for a visit, is the catalyst of the story, serving as the Tiresias figure. His reception is mixed: enthusiastically welcomed by the wife, grudgingly received by the narrator. Bub, as Robert calls the narrator, is mean spirited, asocial, and governed by questionable assumptions about the blind and members of ethnic groups. To his remark that he has no blind friends, his wife responds,

> "You don't have *any* friends." . . .
> I didn't answer. She'd told me a little about the blind man's wife. Her name was Beulah. Beulah! That's a name for a colored woman.
> "Was his wife a Negro?" I asked. (*Where*, 268)

Although a grown man, Bub is no better informed than the adolescent narrator who must be disabused of a mistaken notion about the world. Carver's way of setting up the theme on the first page is to show how little Bub understands about blindness, then to anticipate the final and central event of the story: "She told me he touched his fingers to every part of her face, her nose—even her neck! She never forgot it. She even tried to write a poem about it. . . . She wrote a poem or two every year, usually after something really important had happened to her. . . . In the poem, she talked about what she had felt at the time, about what went through her mind when the blind man touched her nose and lips" (*Where*, 266–67). This will eventually form one of the harmonious parts of the story, but here, Bub can no more see the point than Oedipus could. He goes on to compound his folly by revealing his contempt for the blind: "Imagine a woman who could never see herself as she was seen in the eyes of her loved one. A woman who could go on day after day and never receive the smallest compliment from her beloved. A woman whose husband could never read the expression on her face, be it misery or something better" (*Where*, 269). One need only recall Oedipus's taunt to Tiresias in order to compare the contempt shared by the two protagonists: "for thee that strength is not, since thou art maimed in ear, and in wit, and in eye."[22] Oedipus and Bub possess full sight, but are blind, while Tiresias and Robert are blind, but can see clearly. As Tiresias warns, "And I tell thee—since thou hast taunted me even with blindness—that thou hast sight, yet seest not" (Sophocles, 380). Ultimately, both will be instructed by the blind.

After dinner, the three of them settle down comfortably in the living room so that Robert and Bub's wife can talk about the past 10 years. When Bub thinks they are about through discussing old times and the intervening years, he turns the television on. She leaves to change into her robe, and Bub invites the blind, middle-aged man to smoke marijuana with him. Returning to find them smoking, Bub's wife joins them, but soon falls asleep.

The two men give their attention to a program about the church in the Middle Ages, Bub watching, Robert listening, one ear turned toward the set, as Bub attempts to explain what a cathedral is, but discovers he cannot express what he sees. Undaunted, Robert suggests some heavy paper to draw on. As Bub draws, Robert places his hand over Bub's drawing hand. When the picture is finished, he runs his fingers over the lines. Then he has Bub close his eyes and continue drawing:

> So we kept on with it. His fingers rode my fingers as my hand went over the paper. It was like nothing else in my life up to now.
> Then he said, "I think that's it. I think you got it," he said. "Take a look. What do you think?"
> But I had my eyes closed. I thought I'd keep them that way for a little longer. I thought it was something I ought to do.
> "Well?" he said. "Are you looking?"
> My eyes were still closed. I was in my house. I knew that. But I didn't feel like I was inside anything.
> "It's really something," I said. (*Where*, 279)

Thus, in a replication of his wife's much earlier experience, the narrator discovers the refutation of his assumptions about the blind and seeing. We can imagine the shape of the cathedral materializing before his inner eye as he learns that conventional vision is not the only way to see things and that the eyes are not the only organs with which one can view the world. We can also see that he has not quite grasped the meaning of his experience, but he has acknowledged that special quality his wife experienced and tried to recapture in a poem when he says, "It's really something."

To express such a lesson would be didactic and the worst possible way of developing the theme, not only sentimentalizing the story, but also rendering Bub more articulate than he is. Bub never seems to notice that his experience is identical to his wife's; the discovery is left to our powers of inference. Moreover, in the context of the smoking, Carver allows for a belief on Bub's part that the *something* he experiences is an effect of the marijuana. And therein lies Carver's success.

Although Bub, like his wife 10 years before when she let Robert feel her face, receives a profound, perhaps a character-altering, experience, it would be too much to conclude from what has passed that he experiences a conversion like the baker's in "A Small, Good Thing." Nothing suggests that he will have any more friends from this point on or be governed any less by such spurious notions as, for example, blind people don't smoke because they can't see the smoke. What we can conclude, though, is that he will view from now on his wife's experience in a manner different from his initial attitude, that his attitude toward Robert will be wholly different also, and that he has experienced an event that has the power to trigger the imagination.

With all of his imperfections, Bub remains thoroughly realistic, not a symbol in a modern allegory. We can believe him when he says, "My wife finally took her eyes off the blind man and looked at me. I had the feeling she didn't like what she saw" (*Where*, 270). However, there is the indisputable sense that she may well like what she sees after Robert departs, for in a single event her husband has moved considerably closer to sharing her values—intuitively perhaps, unconsciously, but also convincingly.

"Fever"

Carver's next story, "Fever," is not written with characteristic detachment. It sinks into domestic melodrama and suffers from comparison with "Cathedral" or, for that matter, with other works possessing the same theme: creative illness as initiating premise. Grounded in ancient shamanistic practice, wherein the shaman induces an ecstatic trance during which he divines the hidden, the theme has served literary texts well in the past, most notably Thomas Mann's *Doctor Faustus*. In that ambitious novel, Adrian Leverkuhn's syphilis produces musical genius, but here, as the source of the protagonist's resigned acceptance of his circumstances, the creative illness falls short.

Carlyle is the protagonist. His wife has left him and their children. As a teacher off for the summer, he manages to handle the domestic responsibilities for that period, but with school starting up again, he hires a sitter for the children. When she neglects them and behaves in an unacceptable manner, he is forced to let her go.

That is his quandary when his wife calls from California to let him know she and the man she is with have been working on Carlyle's problem, presumably known to them by extrasensory perception, and have called a Mrs. Webster to come to his aid. An unlikely coincidence, it brings the crucial Mrs. Webster into the story. She takes over the duties. All seems resolved: "That afternoon he arrived home to find his house neat and orderly and his children in clean clothes. In the kitchen, Keith and Sarah stood on chairs, helping Mrs. Webster with gingerbread cookies. Sarah's hair was out of her face and held back with a barrette" (*Where*, 238).

Chaos has been banished; order is restored and symbolized in the children's behavior and the little girl's combed hair. But there must be conflict to make a story. Six weeks pass and all is fine until Carlyle becomes ill. Although Carlyle's wife has not called during the intervening six weeks, she contacts him now, saying that she knows he is sick—another incredible coincidence. Referring to Colette's having kept an account during one of her illnesses, Eileen urges Carlyle to keep a journal of his illness, too.

Apparently, she has a vague idea about creative illnesses and imagines that he is experiencing one. In such ordeals, the sufferer experiences painful symptoms accompanied by a dominating preoccupation. The sickness ends in a state of exhilaration, from which the sufferer emerges with a sense of permanent change and the marked conviction that a great truth has been discovered.

That is exactly what Carver is aiming for, but the wife makes an unconvincing medium for introducing the event. Nevertheless, the transformation occurs. Coming out of his illness, Carlyle learns that Mrs. Webster and her husband are going to move on to help her husband's son by an earlier marriage. This knowledge appears to break the barrier, and he begins to talk, telling her about the early years of his relation with Eileen, their love, their hopes, now lost.

He talks until his lingering headache vanishes, but he does not stop then. He continues even after his children come in and fall asleep on the floor, even after Mr. Webster comes in and quietly takes a chair. He talks everything out of his system in a burst of cathartic confession. As she and her husband are leaving, Mrs. Webster says that she will see him the next morning:

> As if something important had been settled, Carlyle said, "Right!"
> The old couple went carefully along the walk and got into their truck. . . . It was then, as he stood at the window, that he felt something had come to an end. It had to do with Eileen and the life before this. . . . But he understood it was over, and he felt able to let her go. . . . [I]t was something that had passed. And that passing—though it had seemed impossible and he'd fought against it—would become a part of him now, too, as surely as anything else he'd left behind. (*Where*, 247)

Although "Fever" is one of the longest stories in *Cathedral*, it is less developed than some of the shorter ones. Yes, there are crises—not having a sitter, for example, and the illness of the protagonist—but these are not quite convincing as crises, even though they are refracted through the consciousness of a man whose emotional life is a mess. Perhaps they are unconvincing because of Eileen's incredible intervention in each of the crises. One is hard-pressed to justify Eileen's clairvoyance on aesthetic grounds. Unlike Nelson's in "Vitamins" or Robert's in "Cathedral," hers seems forced, although Carver steeps it in New Age trappings and attempts to place it contextually, as he successfully does in the other two stories. Still, the attempt comes off as unjustified and unconvincing coincidence. Moreover, the use of a cathartic illness to resolve a problem or, as is often the case, to reveal mutual feelings of love is a cliché that could benefit from a rest.

Finally, Carlyle's current girlfriend, Carol, seems to have no organic place in the story. She functions as a foil for Carlyle's moods, sympathetic to his sitter crisis, offering to succor him during the crisis, then benefiting from his elation when Mrs. Webster brings order to his life. It is true that her presence helps to slow down the pace of the story, but even in that function, she seems to be misplaced, not there when her presence might hold off the illness for a little while longer and improve the pace of the story. Instead, Carver gives her a brief section in bed with Carlyle immediately before using summary for the transition to the sickness.

"Where I'm Calling From"

When the narrator of "Where I'm Calling From" makes friends with a fellow alcoholic at Frank Martin's drying-out facility, he encourages his new friend to talk about his life, perhaps to keep his mind off his own problems. It turns out his narrator is one of those people who cannot face problems with aplomb. For example, although he thinks about calling his girlfriend, whose Pap smear results led to the binge that brought him to Frank Martin's, he cannot muster the courage to do it: "I hope she's okay. But if she has something wrong with her, I don't want to know about it" (*Where*, 218).

J.P., the narrator's new acquaintance, has an interesting history. He chose to become a chimney sweep because of a fortuitous meeting with Roxy, a female chimney sweep, toward the end of his teens. She arrives at the house J.P. is visiting and, after completing her task and receiving payment, asks the owner of the house if he would like to kiss her for luck. Embarrassed, J.P.'s friend kisses her on the cheek. Spurred suddenly, J.P. decides to ask for a kiss too, then follows her out to her truck, where he says he wants to take her out. Eventually they start working together and marry. She stops working, has children, and they are happy until J.P.'s drinking increases to the point that it becomes a problem. Fights follow. She takes a boyfriend. J.P. loses his driver's license and cannot drive the truck to work. Circumstances reach an unacceptable level, forcing Roxy's father and brother to take J.P. to Frank Martin's.

The narrator, who is already there for the second time, watches as J.P is brought in. He also observes Roxy when she comes to see J.P. on New Year's Day, asking if she can take her husband to lunch. He responds, "I think they'd like it if I didn't leave the place for a little while yet" (*Where*, 219). The sense this response produces is that J.P. values his life with Roxy and is determined to free himself from drinking, unlike the narrator on his first visit to the facility. The first time he was there, a part of him wanted help, but there was another part that did not.

What follows suggests a recognition in the narrator that J.P.'s kiss of the chimney sweep 12 years before has brought him luck, in spite of the problems, for as they start inside, he stops them, saying, "I need some luck. . . . No kidding. I could do with a kiss myself" (*Where*, 219). Roxy tells him she is no longer a sweep, has not been for years, but then she takes him by the shoulders, kisses him on the mouth, and wishes him luck.

The kiss leaves him shaking and thinking about a time years before when a noise outside the house woke him one morning. As he went to the window, his wife informed him that it was the landlord, there to paint the house before the sun got too high. He pulled back the curtain, and the two men stood staring at each other until he realized he was naked and became aware that his wife was calling him back to bed.

Roxy's kiss marks a turning point, as if by asking for the kiss of luck he is acknowledging his condition and is willing to change it. The story closes with the narrator's intention to call his wife, then his girlfriend, implying that he, too, is ready to face the hard choices. Now, for the first time, he is able to confront his girlfriend's worst news, if not with aplomb, at least with courage.

The distinction between place and condition that the title "Where I'm Calling From" seems to enforce is not real. Taking pains to emphasize shared elements among the residents at Frank Martin's drying-out facility, Carver constructs a metaphor of condition from the particulars of place. No summary can do the story justice because it is a narrative that depends not on a causal chain of events for its value, but on the subtle development of character, and as has been pointed out before, one of the ways Carver informs readers is to use parallel and opposite characters as commentary on a protagonist's condition.

Three characters—J.P., Tiny, and a man who denies his drinking problem—function in this manner. Each possesses elements in common with the narrator, elements beyond their alcoholism and presence at the facility. The narrator gives his attention to bodily signs, his own and those of others at the drying-out facility. For example, while observing J.P., the narrator dwells on and identifies with Tiny, fearing that his own twitches could signal a seizure. It is clear that he also has practiced denial, not facing his girlfriend's possible cancer or in the past his own alcoholism. Ultimately, however, these fears and refusals cease to paralyze him.

"Where I'm Calling From" is one of several fictions in *Cathedral* that, when taken as a whole, create the book's overall feeling of generosity. By comparing the three commercial collections, the sympathetic reader can see how strikingly this book differs from the earlier collections, but it might be helpful to mention related stories from the three collections and observe Carver's movement toward a state of greater generosity toward his characters and maturity. Characters possess more positive qualities. There is less unrelieved misery.

Early in Carver's first collection of fiction, the narrator of "Fat" has an imaginative experience that is shared with, but not understood or appreciated by, her friend Rita. Then with the publication of his second commercial collection, Carver reverses the situation. In "Sacks," he develops a character who hears his father's story, but fails to grasp the point. Both present examples of limited imagination. Here, however, in a positive variation on the theme, the narrator of "Where I'm Calling From" hears J.P.'s story, is suggestively influenced, and makes the adjustments necessary to recognize his condition.

While the story shares many qualities with earlier stories—for example, its understated and realistic treatment—and possesses the generosity that distinguishes this collection, it should be added that its achievement is free from the melodrama and sentimentality that mark "A Small, Good Thing" and "Fever." Further evidence of its worth can be found in its selection for *The Best American Short Stories, 1983* and in the fact that Carver decided to use its title for his last collection of selected and new fiction.

Mastery and Continued Growth:
Where I'm Calling From

If *Cathedral* can be viewed as an index to the aesthetics of the eighties, a snapshot of American tastes during that period, no such unqualified claim can be made for *Where I'm Calling From: New and Selected Stories* (1988). The last book of stories published during his life, it evenly represents fiction spanning two and a half decades of writing—that which came before *Cathedral*, a transitional collection itself, and that which followed it—and sums up a life of fiction writing. However, since selections from *Cathedral* and the work that followed it make up half the volume, *Where I'm Calling From* reflects the cultural changes of Carver's last decade and his "belief in, and love for, the things of this world" (McCaffery, 64).

The new stories that round off the volume also reveal his continued growth and vigor. Previous fine writers lost their productive vitality because resistance to change prevented a renewal of their talents. Unlike the creative powers of many twentieth-century American writers—Hemingway's, Capote's, Tennessee Williams's—Carver's did not diminish at the end. He was still expanding his boundaries beyond what had been achieved in the early decades of writing.

Two developments illustrate and underscore this new growth. The first is the transition during his last years from blue-collar fictionist to full-fledged writer for the *New Yorker,* where all but two of his final stories were published. The second development that testifies to his capacity for renewal, perhaps as compensation for concessions to class appeal, can be found in an aesthetic boldness that begins to manifest itself in the penultimate and final stories of *Where I'm Calling From.* The expressionism of "Blackbird Pie" and imagined history of "Errand," for example, signal a striking departure from the old, for which very little in Carver's realistic fiction could have prepared us.

A transition from literary to popular magazines customarily compromises the aesthetics of one's work. Similar shifts by John O'Hara, Irwin Shaw, and Mario Puzo offer exemplary lessons about the critical hazards of acceding to popular demands. Such was not the case with Carver, however. Without relinquishing the high standards he had established over the years, he was able to adapt to the requirements of the *New Yorker* in a number of ways.

One concession can be found in a "willingness to seek his characters outside the lower classes," according to Mark Facknitz in "Raymond Carver and the Menace of Minimalism" (Facknitz, 68). Another—and it is appropriate for his educated, well-to-do characters when they appear—is his willingness to forgo the highly stylized grammatical constructions, repetitions, truncated syntax, and other features that make his work recognizable. The key clause, however, is *when they appear,* for much of his last work remains consistent with the early stories.

"Intimacy"

> "Gathering Leaves" (that saddest, most-carefully-unspecified symbol for our memories)
>
> —Randall Jarrell, *Poetry and the Age*[23]

The leaves of autumn in literature have traditionally reminded us of that for which we grieve—lost youth, lost love, lost times—and Carver's late fiction makes use of this tradition, but with a twist. In his work, leaves also engender guilt, becoming the representation of essential matters we cannot afford to neglect, but nonetheless do: "Your work became more important, and our time together was squeezed out," the departing wife writes in "Blackbird Pie" (*Where,* 367). Looking at the leaves in the gutter and underfoot at the end of "Intimacy," the narrator says, "Somebody ought to get a rake and take care of this" (*Where,* 337), as if these leaves are the scattered remnants of an intimacy that could be gathered up and restored or, at least, put into some sort of order. As metaphors of grief and guilt over failed responsibilities, fallen leaves unite "Intimacy" and "Menudo," two stories that hark back to Carver's early fiction and to what the unnamed narrator of the first story calls "the dark view of things" (*Where,* 334).

When he appears unannounced one morning at the home of his former wife, she immediately embarks on a tirade in language remarkably similar to that of the departing wife in "Blackbird Pie." Juxtaposing excerpts from the stories, the reader is hard-pressed to distinguish one wife from the other:

And you know what I'm talking about. . . . Even after we were married we used to talk and talk. . . . When the children were little . . . we still found time to talk. It was more difficult . . . but we managed, we found time. We *made* time. . . . Sometimes we'd engage a sitter just so we *could* talk. (*Where*, 367)

We were so *intimate* once upon a time I can't believe it now. I think that's the strangest thing of all now. The memory of being that intimate with somebody. We were so intimate I could puke. I can't imagine ever being that intimate with somebody else. . . . You know what I'm talking about, don't you? (*Where*, 333)

The narrator is a writer, and because he has sent her items written by or about him during the four years they have not seen each other, she is aware that he exploits the shards of their devastated life. Now that he has shown up without warning, his appearance provides an opportunity to complain about the anguish and humiliation he causes by revealing "the low, shameful things" (*Where*, 333) of their intimacy: "Then you held me up for display and ridicule in your so-called work. For any Tom or Harry to pity or pass judgment on. Ask me if I cared. Ask me if it embarrassed me. Go ahead, ask" (*Where*, 335). It is a betrayal, and she wants it to stop: "Frankly, and I mean this, I want to be kept out of it from here on out" (*Where*, 332–33).

She is so concerned about his motives that, when he acknowledges her long ago threat with a knife and encourages her to tell him about it, she begins to suspect he has come for more details: "I think I know why you're here. Yes, I know why you're here, even if you don't. But you're a slyboots. You know why you're here. You're on a fishing expedition. You're hunting for *material*. Am I getting warm? Am I right?" (*Where*, 333).

The rancor, suspicion, and stream of accusatory clichés testify to the gaping emotional wound she suffers. Insisting that he has been confusing himself with the person about whom the articles are written (thus pronouncing the paradox of the writer as public figure and the writer as existential individual), invoking her right to privacy, and citing her own identity crisis, she touches the quick of his conscience. For he is a troubled man, spiritually less than whole. He goes to his knees and, like the diseased men of Gennesaret seeking wholeness by touching the hem of Christ's garment, grasps the hem of her dress, refusing to let go. It is in such gestures that Marilynne Robinson finds "the germ of myth and archetype" within Carver's fiction.[24]

His act also reminds us of Jacob refusing to release the angel until he is blessed. "It's crazy, but I'm still on my knees holding the hem of her dress. I won't let go. I'm like a terrier, and it's like I'm stuck to the floor. It's like I can't move" (*Where*, 336).

Only after she forgives him, giving him dispensation "to tell it like you have to, I guess, and forget the rest" (*Where*, 337), does he relinquish his hold, but she has no expectation that their strange reconciliation will last: "This'll wear off, you know. Pretty soon you'll start feeling bad again. Maybe it'll make a good story, she says. But I don't want to know about it if it does" (*Where*, 337). As he departs, the image of fallen leaves fills his thoughts: "There are these leaves everywhere, even in the gutters. Piles of leaves wherever I look. They're falling off the limbs as I walk. I can't take a step without putting my shoe into leaves. Somebody ought to make an effort here. Somebody ought to get a rake and take care of this" (*Where*, 337).

The emotional content latent beneath the stream of clichés and the narrator's mute gesture of going to his knees before his former wife, reaching out for the hem of her dress, differs profoundly from the easier redemption of "A Small, Good Thing." Here in "Intimacy," characters do not possess adequate words for the raw emotion they feel. She has only ready-made expressions; he is limited to his gesture of supplication. And yet, despite their limitations, we feel the tension between these flesh-and-blood characters, and it has the power to move us emotionally.

Most critics will agree with Mark Facknitz that "Intimacy" revisits the fiction of earlier periods. While many may also share his conclusion that such a return shows "Carver . . . indulging himself in a kind of torpid kookiness that characterized *Will You Please Be Quiet, Please?* and *What We Talk about When We Talk about Love*" (Facknitz, 67–68), some will not. Instead, they will find in "Intimacy" the earned sentiment that is missing from "A Small, Good Thing" and a germinal myth more imaginatively incorporated than is the myth of redemption in that story.

"Menudo"

As the narrator of "Intimacy" passes on, his mind full of leaves that need raking, Hughes draws us into "Menudo" and focuses our attention on "leaves heaped up under the front windows" of Amanda Porter's house across the street (*Where*, 338) so that although the story lines are not literally connected, we sense the transition and the link. It is a time of crisis. His affair with Amanda has brought him to another turning point in a life of such junctures. Oliver Porter, having discovered his wife's infidelity, has left and told her to be gone when he returns. The development, a few days before, was threatening enough to drive Hughes into a frenzy of gathering and bagging leaves. By morning, he will rake the yard once again, as well as the neighbors' yard, and the narrative will end as he crosses the street to rake Amanda's yard. Like the narrator of "Intimacy," he thinks someone should take care of the leaves.

Before morning, during this night of insomnia, Hughes will recall events in a life characterized by avoidance and a compulsive appetite for personal disaster. Indeed, the personal disasters, his adultery, his alcoholism, his compulsiveness may result from his need to avoid unpleasant realities. Certainly, the evidence suggests as much.

Married to a woman whose dress, manner, and talk indicate the onset of mental illness, he turns to another woman. Discovering the affair, his wife slips beyond acceptable behavior and is institutionalized, causing Hughes to bolt from the marriage, frightened. While she is hospitalized, he avoids her, refusing to visit her or even to write.

The pattern persists in his relations with the second wife. Instead of dealing with his wife's infidelity when he learns of her affair, he takes to his bed, thus avoiding once again having to confront the situation and its implications. When his unstable mother makes it clear that she would like a radio, he ignores, then refuses, her wish, and during his avoidance, his mother dies. Finally, in the current crisis, he reveals again his desire to avoid confrontation by asking Amanda, "You didn't admit who it was you were involved with, did you?" (*Where*, 339).

Unable to sleep, Hughes is alone with these memories of emotional underdevelopment, unsupported by any firm beliefs, no longer relying on alcohol to soften the jagged edges of his life, reliving a memory of an event at a party. With his first wife in the institution, he remembers he was at the party, drinking, no doubt attempting to blot out the circumstances of his life, although he believed he no longer cared what happened. He is drunk in the kitchen when the shakes overtake him.

His host, Alfredo, takes one look at his condition and prescribes menudo, a traditional Mexican tripe dish. Hughes sits there, shaking in the kitchen, watching Alfredo put in the ingredients, the chorizo, garlic, and peppercorns, the chili powder, salt, and lemon juice, the white bread, tomato sauce, and hominy. He watches Alfredo as he cooks and talks, but Hughes understands nothing that is said. Then, suddenly, he goes into a spare room and passes out. When he wakes late the next day, the people and the menudo are gone. He has missed out on the menudo.

It seems an insignificant thing to remember, but the facts of his life can be reduced to this one event. He has missed out. Avoiding strange, uncomfortable, and painful realities through alcohol, extramarital relations, and denial, he never experiences life in ways that might help him develop. That has been his condition, and that condition will persist. For as day breaks, he returns to the yard and to gathering leaves. It is one more act of compulsive avoidance, and there is nothing in the story to suggest he will break the pattern of errors and compulsion as he resorts to that saddest, most-carefully-unspecified symbol for his memories: gathering leaves.

"Boxes"

Hughes's uncomfortable relationship with his neurotic mother appears as only a troubled memory of affection withheld until it is too late, one in a series of missed opportunities that characterize him. As an undeveloped element in the mosaic of his life, its potential unexploited, it serves the purpose of contributing to the finished portrait. However, the potential does not escape Carver, for he develops a similar relationship between son and mother in "Boxes."

For half a year after her decision to move back to California, the narrator's mother has lived among her packed boxes in the town of Longview, putting off the move that will certify her solitude. As long as she remains in the same town with her son, the pretense can continue in spite of her evident dissatisfaction. She finds fault with the town. She finds fault with her landlord. She finds fault with the weather and a great deal more, but she never finds fault with herself.

Her history, with her late husband and after, consists of repeated, futile moves in search of happiness. She is among a host of Carver's rootless characters, moving from place to place, living in rented houses, apartments, trailer parks, and motor courts. Socially and spiritually immobile, they take to the road, moving horizontally in a world that denies them upward mobility and daily reminds them that home ownership is the American dream. When she announced her intention to move from California to Longview where her son lives, he tried to discourage her with reasons that, however valid, revealed his unwillingness to make her a part of his life. Undeterred, she made the move and set into motion her most recent unhappiness, which manifests itself in stratagems for attention. Her hope that they would go on picnics and take drives together never comes to pass.

And now it is June. They have a final meal together, and afterward, it occurs to the son that he will never see his mother again. Two days later, she returns to California and, a few days later, calls to say she is settled. During the conversation, she begins to list her new complaints about the manager, the California traffic and weather, the air-conditioning in her apartment. She hopes she has not made a mistake in moving back.

At this moment the son remembers the affectionate expression his father used when addressing his wife. It is *dear*. As a youngster, he had been soothed by it as a source of hope for the future. He says the word, unable to think of anything else to go with it, as if all meaning resides in the word alone. He repeats it to his mother before he can finally muster his thought enough to add, "Dear, try not to be afraid" (*Where*, 316). Then he says he loves her and will write.

Reminiscent of the understated gestures in Carver's early fiction, this strikingly small and pessimistic concession to emotion is all the son can muster, and yet, reduced to a single word, the expression speaks forcefully of the loss and loneliness and pathos, both the mother's and the son's. This is a menace quite different from that which Carver evokes in "Vitamins." It is the silent scream of those who search and cannot find, those who feel but cannot express.

"Intimacy," "Menudo," and "Boxes" are holdovers from a fictional vision that makes many uneasy as it tracks through the squalor of adultery, alcoholism, and self-deception, focusing on women in curlers, door-to-door salesmen trying to make a pitch to the unemployed, bankrupts, and lonely neurotics. Its method is to show the surface of things by lingering on observable facts without commentary and staging tiny dramas between people as we find them. The surface becomes everything, suggesting the inner person who often possesses no available past or one strewn with error and chaos. Not all who leave this fictional world queasy are casual readers, for it can unsettle even the toughest critic; but it is no less valuable for that.

Fortunately, for readers who prefer upbeat fiction, Carver ranges into less pessimistic areas and, in so doing, has reached a broader readership. His new work strikes out boldly, going well beyond even the extended boundaries of "Cathedral." Indeed, "Cathedral" should be seen as a transition to the final type, the linchpin that locks the early fiction to "Blackbird Pie" and "Errand."

"Blackbird Pie"

Prior to the textured boldness of "Blackbird Pie," Carver's body of writing was for the most part free from literary experimentation, and his public stance over the years concerning such activity was less than enthusiastic. In the McCaffery-Gregory interview he says, "I'm not interested in works which are all texture and no flesh-and-blood" (McCaffery, 75). Nevertheless, in the same interview, his acknowledgment of Donald Barthelme's "*world* of work" reveals an autumnal tolerance, an openness characteristic of maturity and self-confidence: "I didn't care much for [Barthelme's work] when I first started reading it. It seemed so strange that I stopped reading him for a while. . . . But then I read *Sixty Stories* a couple of years ago. He's terrific! I found that the more I read his stories the more regard I began to have for them. Barthelme has done a *world* of work" (McCaffery, 76).

The openness and revised judgment result from a self-assured posture that nurtures curiosity, emboldens one to attempt unexpected effects, and ultimately leads to unanticipated forms. As Facknitz notes, "'Blackbird Pie' and 'Errand' . . . seem to mark a new and more sophisticated tendency" (Facknitz, 68). The title "Blackbird Pie," referring us to the nursery rhyme "Sing a Song of Sixpence," and the tension between the plainly stated facts of that story and the narrator's incredulity about the events are an approving nod toward Barthelme (who built a complete literary world from reinvented fairy tales, legends, nursery rhymes, popular culture, and surrealism) and toward the expressionism of Kafka.

Recalling that expressionism is best understood as a reaction against realism—with objects and events appearing as if in a dream, a distorted, even nightmarish vision of reality—we have reason to be surprised at its appearance in the work of a writer as closely identified with realism as Carver.

Like "the king . . . in his countinghouse / Counting out his money," the narrator of "Blackbird Pie" retires to his study after the evening meal. While sequestered, he observes a thick envelope slide under the door. It is addressed to him, purports to be from his wife, and contains the grievances of 23 years together. However, the narrator claims that it is in the handwriting of someone other than his wife and that it is out of keeping with her character.

Carver fuses traditionally antithetical elements by contrasting matter-of-fact details with a strange, dreamlike indefiniteness, which gives the narrative an uncanny effect. For example, a letter purportedly written by his wife is slipped under his door, but he denies that it is in her handwriting. The result draws attention to the distance between the narrator and the implied author. As more assertions are made, the narrator's unreliability becomes increasingly apparent, undercutting his authority.

He makes a claim for his superior memory, but cannot remember what happened to the letter. He confuses the common expression "as easy as pie" with "simple as blackbird pie. The famous four and twenty that were set before the king" (*Where*, 366). He insists he can remember every word of what he reads, but reproduces only a fragment of the letter, claiming to have stopped reading after one and a half paragraphs. On the basis of such evidence, Facknitz observes that "Carver uses a distinctly antiminimalist voice, the only clear instance in his work when he distinguishes between narrator and implied author" (Facknitz, 68).

On the evening his wife chooses for her departure, a fog rolls in, creating an unreal atmosphere and profound doubts about what is being experienced, and with the fog come two horses grazing at the front door. Soon a deputy sheriff and a rancher arrive, and the rancher takes his horses and the narrator's wife away.

Full of sexual symbolism, the story possesses the logic of a dream in which bizarre, inexplicable events occur. The narrator, emotionally distracted by his wife's departure and all the implications of sexual inadequacy that that situation entails, summons up images from "Sing a Song of Sixpence," with its "Along came a blackbird / And snipped off her nose," a memory that leads through an associational matrix to more arcane recollections about the "infamous Ali Muezzin Zade, a man who was fond of personally cutting off the noses of his prisoners before calling in the executioners" (*Where*, 366).

At first, the evocation of "Sing a Song of Sixpence" and the unexpected recollection of a tyrant who capriciously cuts off the noses of his prisoners seem limited to the narrator's disoriented state in which any nonsense might pop into the character's head. However, such references should not be written off as mere mannerisms without deeper implications, for any obsession with severed limbs must be seen in a

Freudian context, where it will be interpreted as a classic fear of castration, especially if the situation features a character losing his wife.

When the focus narrows to severed noses, the theme of emasculation becomes even more pronounced than usual. For literature is rife with explicit links between the nose and the genitals: for example, in Rabelais's *Gargantua and Pantagruel;* in Laurence Sterne's *Tristram Shandy;* and in Mikhail Bakhtin's assertions "that [the nose] always symbolizes the phallus" and that the "most widely known example of this symbolism is the famous carnival 'Dance of the Noses' of Hans Sachs (*Nasentanz*)" (Bakhtin, 316). Bakhtin also traces the tradition to earlier periods: "In both antique and medieval grotesque the nose had usually this link with the phallus" (Bakhtin, 87).

What seems incoherent is harmonious after all, forming an appropriate logic for the story. Just as an abandoned husband can suffer from anxieties about his virility, so too a foggy atmosphere and bizarre events might cause a character to express his obsessions in the language of dreams, where images take on symbolic implications, for in the depths of the unconscious exists a nexus of rich images that juxtaposes severed noses and powerful, vital horses.

The preoccupation with emasculation is not new in Carver. It formed a crucial point in his first nationally published story, "Pastoral" (republished in *Fires* as "The Cabin"). Readers will recall the distress of Mr. Harrold when his illusions of manliness are destroyed by the younger generation. They should also recall that losing his fishing rod, with its attendant sexual implications, completes his sense of inadequacy.

Carver's beleaguered narrator in "Blackbird Pie" watches as his wife is drawn to the horses that appear mysteriously out of the fog. He must endure her suggestive touching and nuzzling, her terms of endearment, her emotional reaction, her crooning. The power of the animals stands opposed to the severed noses: "She was standing beside this big horse, patting its flank. . . . Then she moved forward and put her face against the horse's mane. . . . My wife moved with the horse, hanging on to its mane. I put my hand against the horse's neck and felt a surge of power run up my arm to the shoulder" (*Where*, 373).

When the deputy sheriff and the rancher show up, it is impossible to dismiss the implied comparison between the horses and these two western men with their trappings of virility: "Then a big man in a raincoat got out of the car. . . . But his raincoat was open, and I could see a pistol strapped to his waist" (*Where*, 374). The scene increases the narrator's anxiety as he finds "it *worth noting* that both men were wearing hats" (*Where*, 374). With his wife and the two men wearing hats, his uncovered state suggests an exposed vulnerability and emphasizes his difference. Here on his own doorstep, he is the outsider, helpless and forced to watch as his wife leaves with the rancher.

However, more important than any loss of sexual power is the narrator's final sense of historical loss, which calls his very existence into question. If it is a dream, his existence may depend entirely on the dreamer—or, as he puts it, on his wife's writing more letters or telling a friend who keeps a diary: "Then, years later, someone can look back on this time, interpret it according to the record, its scraps and tirades, its silences and innuendos" (*Where*, 380). Arriving at this conclusion, the narrator anticipates "Errand" and Carver's final word on history and writing as a confirmation of one's existence.

"Errand"

"Errand" bears witness to what can be achieved when one follows Paul Valéry's example of "The Method of Leonardo." He asserts in his essay on da Vinci that "very little . . . I shall have to say of [Leonardo da Vinci] should be applied to the man who made this name illustrious":

> An author who *composes* a biography can try to *live* his subject or else to *construct* him, and there is a decided opposition between these two courses. *To live him* is to transform oneself into what is necessarily incomplete, since life in this sense is composed of anecdotes, details, moments. *Construction*, on the other hand, implies the *a priori* conditions of an existence that could be *completely different.*
>
> This sort of logic is what leads by way of sensory impressions to the construction of what I have just called a *universe.*[25]

What Carver constructs by way of sensory impressions in "Errand" is an imaginary universe that is all his own, a *world* like the one he attributed to Barthelme. Refusing to find the major factors of a life in the usual documentation, his biography becomes a fiction.

Although this development can be demonstrated by analysis and explication and by citing expert testimony, the radical nature of it is more forcefully illustrated by Mark Helprin, who chose the stories for *The Best American Stories, 1988.* In his introduction, Helprin explains that "the stories in this volume have been judged blindly. Shannon Ravenel graciously blacked out the names of the authors, and my wife went even further and blacked out the names of the publications. Of course we could not have obliterated characteristic graphics, styles, and voices, but I confess that the voices were not familiar to me and that therefore no one was afforded advantage or suffered disadvantage."[26]

The method works to Helprin's satisfaction. Upon learning he has selected stories by individuals whose work he usually finds intolerable, he is pleasantly shocked, a revelation that might leave readers bemused were it not for an unambiguous and passionate detailing of his biases with regard to literature. He loves literature that is "pleasingly beautiful" and "deeply consequential" (Helprin, xiv). He reports that he does not like minimalist fiction littered with brand names and people in ill health, who watch television and are addicted to tobacco, alcohol, and coffee. Nor does he like characters without professions or trades (Helprin, xxiii–xxiv).

The items on this list, he informs the reader, are the "useless touchstones of American fiction" (Helprin, xxiv), an attitude Chekhov anticipated when he created Burkin and Alehin, who "felt inclined, for some reason, to talk about elegant people" and were not satisfied with the dreary story of a clerk who ate gooseberries.[27] The items are also touchstones of the fiction on which Raymond Carver built his early reputation.

Nevertheless, Helprin selected Carver's "Errand" despite tuberculosis, waiters, brand names (Moët), insomnia, and the use of tobacco, coffee, and alcohol. Although this lapse may be a consequence of Helprin's kinder attitude toward waiters attending well-fed bankers and rosy-cheeked tourists among the jars of caviar and bottles of champagne at a fashionable watering place, it is more likely explained by Carver's radical departure from his earlier fiction.

For in "Errand," both form and content have been altered. Characteristic signatures of plain diction and disrupted syntax, those recognizable markers of Carver's voice, are absent, replaced by the language of the traditional historian: "Waiters came and went ceaselessly" (*Where*, 381); "impressed with the solicitude shown" (*Where*, 383); "without conferring" (*Where*, 385); "so entirely appropriate it seems inevitable" (*Where*, 386). Having adopted the historian's voice, Carver maintains it to the end. This is the language we expect from characters who frequent exclusive resorts, and Badenweiler in the western area of the Black Forest, with the Vosges in sight, is a long way from Hopelessville and blue-collar despair.

And yet, other characteristic markers are present. The story focuses on one of Carver's earliest and most persistent themes: the imaginative leap occurring in the mind of one character, its absence in another, both of whom are present at the same time and place. We may recall the narrator of "Fat" and her friend Rita, as an example.

Helprin characterizes the story as a "cold and brilliant imagining of the death of Chekhov" (Helprin, xxx), and Facknitz calls it a "biographical fantasy on the death of Anton Chekhov" (Facknitz, 68). They mean the author's imaginative realization, but the imagination is at once shaper, subject, and product, exemplifying that old triptych of signifier, signified, and signification.

The story opens on the night of 22 March 1897 and a dinner for Chekhov and his friend Alexei Suvorin at the Heritage. The trappings are posh, but the 10-course meal, including wines, liqueurs, coffee, is interrupted when Chekhov begins to hemorrhage. Chekhov's illness is introduced in a page, followed by a summarizing transition that carries the reader to 1904 and Badenweiler, a German spa. Relying on passages from Suvorin's diary, Maria Chekhov's *Memoirs*, Tolstoy's journal, Chekhov's own writings, and especially Henri Troyat's biography of Chekhov, Carver provides hospital impressions, the extent of Chekhov's illness, and the fact of Chekhov's marriage to Olga Knipper, a distinguished actress.

Except for the initial word of the story—"Chekhov," which stands alone—"Errand" is written in the articulate idiom of the historian with complete sentences, elevated diction, scholarly coherence, and omniscient authority. It moves forward over a span of time, space, and action to the crucial night of Chekhov's death, and here Carver's fictive touch becomes visible. All that has gone before is necessary exposition, which establishes the historian's voice, but without negating the work's fictionality.

In his introduction to *Prize Stories 1988: The O. Henry Awards*, William Abrahams discusses "Errand" as the first prize story and deals quickly with the notion that real people cannot appear in fiction: "The biographical details around which the story has been composed will be found in any biography. But almost at once Carver strikes a note of his own."[28] That last statement reminds us that *fiction* derives from *fingere*, the Latin verb for the act of *shaping*, and that striking one's own note is the defining activity.

Both Carver and Troyat freely move the focus from one individual to another. On the night of the great man's death, Olga sends a young

Russian for the doctor. Her memory of the event was striking enough for Troyat to cite it: "I can still hear the sound of the gravel under his shoes in the silence of that stifling July night"[29] and for Carver to reproduce it in his story (*Where*, 385). The image evoked by this historical errand could well be the source of Carver's imaginary errand. In any case, the errand brings the doctor, who injects camphor into Chekhov, but without effect.

It is at this point in the narrative that Carver's dramatic powers begin to draw apart from the biographer's traditional task. Where Troyat writes, "So Dr. Schwöhrer sent for a bottle of champagne" (Troyat, 332), Carver creates a scene and brings it to life with details and dialogue. He invents the expression on the doctor's face, goes into his mind, details the attempt to call down to the kitchen and the conversation. Inspired, he fashions the young man who, roused from his sleep, brings the champagne, going into the detail of the brand name and room number.

The three principal characters take a glass of Moët. Chekhov says it has been a long time since he has tasted champagne. He drinks, turns on his side, and stops breathing. Out of habit, the doctor has pushed the cork back into the bottle. Now he draws a watch, taking Chekhov's wrist, and holds it as the second hand circles the watch face three times. At this moment a black moth flies into the room, striking the lamp, and the doctor releases the wrist, saying, "It's over" (*Where*, 387). As the doctor leaves Olga with her dead husband, the cork pops from the champagne bottle, and foam spills over.

These details—the second hand turning, the memento mori of the black moth flying into the room, the doctor snapping the watch cover down, the cork popping out, and the foam spilling over—are rendered as cinematic images, creating moments of pronounced objective narrative as if only the camera is involved. It is a rare emphasizing of the literary text's cinematic possibilities.

With Chekhov dead, the focus shifts from him to his wife. Olga stays with the deceased until morning when the young man who brought the champagne returns with roses. He wants to retrieve the silver bucket and clear away the glasses. He also wants to announce that breakfast will be served in the garden. Standing there with the roses in his hand, unaware of what has occurred, he sees the cork on the floor.

Suddenly Olga informs him that she needs him to go for the mortician, and here, the omniscient narrator and Olga merge. In a fantasy of the young man's errand, she projects her vision into her instructions, description of what he can expect, and reassurances. One of the great Russian writers has died. His death and embalming must be attended to with the greatest discretion. This is the most important thing ever to happen to the young man, but he is unaware of it. His great concern is for the cork lying at his feet and how to retrieve it while holding a vase of yellow roses.

With unanticipated symmetry, the theme of Carver's last story—the imaginative leap—rejoins that of "Fat," the initial fiction of his first collection, *Will You Please Be Quiet, Please?* We should recall that in "Fat," the narrator-waitress attempts to communicate the extraordinary effect of her encounter with an obese customer by telling her friend about the experience. Unfortunately, the shared event is interpreted in diametric fashion by the two principals—the one heightened by imagination, the other locked on the trivial—so that the event is both significant and trivial without contradiction since it depends on opposed interpretations.

The juxtaposed antithetical attitudes, also repeated in "Sacks," occur in "Errand" with the uncanny effect of a third-person omniscience that narrows the distance between author and character, making it difficult to differentiate between the two. This ambiguity makes Madame Chekhov, not the waiter, the central figure. Her attitude (and the author's), influenced by Chekhov's death, reflects the magnitude of the errand. She, the author, and the reader invest the errand with its special coloring because of her, the author's, and the reader's respective relations with the great man and consequent emotional states.

Never having loved the man or read his work, unaware of the details and consequently the significance, Carver's young waiter is concerned only about the cork at his feet. Although his errand—imagined by Olga or the implied author or both—places the attention on him, it is the act of imagining that has always occupied the central position for Carver. Marilynne Robinson notes this characteristic of Carver's work in her review of *Where I'm Calling From*: "Nothing recurs so powerfully in these stories as the imagination of another life, always so like the narrator's or the protagonist's own that the imagination of it is an experience of the self" (Robinson, 35). She might have added that the imagination of another's life is also a characterizing element: "He was nearly grown-up now and shouldn't be frightened or repelled by any of this" (*Where*, 391). Such a thought directs the angle of vision from Madame Chekhov to the waiter. As a projection of her values, it removes any chance that the image of the young man's errand is his fantasy. "Nearly grown-up" would not fit the self-image of a young man in such a place.

With the passage of time, Carver's stories will sort themselves out, some rising to the top and remaining there, some settling at lower positions on the critical scale. The controversy over minimalism will continue. We can count on that because it lacks the elements for broad appeal. There will also be disagreement about "A Small, Good Thing" because of its sentimentality, although most critics have deflected that criticism. Certainly, that feature and the story's theme of redemption have made it more attractive than "The Bath" with its theme of menace for most readers. Over the transitional stories—"Cathedral," "Blackbird Pie," "Errand"—there should be less contention because, measured against all the fiction Carver wrote, they are truly exceptional, possessing the promise of greater work to come.

Anything but depleted, Carver was fashioning a new world of fiction when he died, bringing to it a freshness that might have redefined "the Carveresque" had he lived longer and continued in the direction he was going. "Cathedral" took a sharp turn away from despair and did so without compromising the hard edge of Carver's earlier work. "Blackbird Pie" dared to go beyond realism. "Errand" was a loving tribute to the writer who traced secure, intact paths for Raymond Carver to follow. He followed them until it was time to break new ground and trace paths of his own, and along those new paths there were markers, possessing a special merit, that identified the course as exclusively Carver's.

Notes to Part 1

1. Cited in Sophie Laffitte, *Chekhov: 1860–1904*, trans. Moura Budberg and Gordon Latta (New York: Charles Scribner's Sons, 1974), 239.

2. Mona Simpson and Lewis Buzbee, "*The Paris Review* Interview," in Raymond Carver, *Fires: Essays, Poems, Stories* (New York: Vintage Books, 1984), 193. Hereafter cited in the text as Simpson. Further references to Carver's work in this volume will be parenthetical (*Fires*).

3. Larry McCaffery and Sinda Gregory, "An Interview with Raymond Carver," *Mississippi Review* 40/41 (Winter 1985): 81. Hereafter cited in the text as McCaffery.

4. Mark A. R. Facknitz, "Raymond Carver and the Menace of Minimalism," *CEA Critic* 52 (Fall 1989/Winter 1990): 62.

5. *Where I'm Calling From: New and Selected Stories* (New York: Atlantic Monthly Press, 1988), xv; hereafter cited in the text as *Where*.

6. Mikhail Bakhtin, *Rabelais and His World*, trans. Hélène Iswolsky (Bloomington: Indiana University Press, 1984), 19; hereafter cited in the text as Bakhtin.

7. Franz Kafka, "A Hunger Artist," in *Selected Stories of Franz Kafka*, trans. Willa and Edwin Muir (New York: Modern Library, 1952), 200.

8. Jonathan Culler, *Structuralist Poetics: Structuralism, Linguistics, and the Study of Literature* (Ithaca: Cornell University Press, 1975), 225.

9. *Will You Please Be Quiet, Please?* (New York: McGraw-Hill Book Company, 1978), 19; hereafter cited in the text as *Will*.

10. Ernest Hemingway, *A Moveable Feast* (New York: Charles Scribner's Sons, 1964), 75.

11. Carlos Baker, *Ernest Hemingway: A Life Story* (New York: Charles Scribner's Sons, 1969), 109; hereafter cited in the text as Baker.

12. *Furious Seasons* (Santa Barbara, Calif.: Capra Press, 1977), 62–63; hereafter cited in the text as *Seasons*.

13. *What We Talk about When We Talk about Love* (New York: Alfred A. Knopf, 1981), 45; hereafter cited in the text as *What*.

14. Oliver Sacks, *The Man Who Mistook His Wife for a Hat and Other Clinical Tales* (New York: Summit Books, 1985), 50–51; hereafter cited in the text as Sacks.

15. Paul Valéry, "The Course in Poetics: First Lesson," trans. Jackson Mathews, in *The Creative Process: A Symposium*, ed. Brewster Ghiselin (New York: New American Library, 1952), 94.

16. Jane Tompkins, *Sensational Designs: The Cultural Work of American Fiction, 1790–1860* (New York: Oxford University Press, 1985), 124; hereafter cited in the text as Tompkins.

17. Michel Foucault, *Madness and Civilization: A History of Insanity in the Age of Reason* (New York: Vintage Books, 1988), 175; hereafter cited in the text as Foucault.

18. Ernest Hemingway, "The Short Happy Life of Francis Macomber," in *The Complete Short Stories of Ernest Hemingway: The Finca Vigía Edition* (New York: Charles Scribner's Sons, 1987), 26.

19. Timothy Harris, *Good Night and Good-bye* (New York: Dell Publishing Company Co., 1979), 147.

20. Isak Dinesen, *Out of Africa* (New York: Quality Paperback Book Club, 1965), 369.

21. *Cathedral* (New York: Alfred A. Knopf, 1984), 208. Further references will be parenthetical (*Cathedral*).

22. Sophocles, *Oedipus the King*, trans. R. C. Jebb, in *The Complete Greek Drama*, ed. Whitney J. Oates and Eugene O'Neill, Jr. (New York: Random House, 1938), 379; hereafter cited in the text as Sophocles.

23. Randall Jarrell, *Poetry and the Age* (New York: Alfred A. Knopf, 1953), 66.

24. Marilynne Robinson, "Marriage and Other Astonishing Bonds," *New York Times Book Review*, 15 May 1988, 35; hereafter cited in the text as Robinson.

25. Paul Valéry, *An Anthology*, selected with an introduction by James R. Lawler (London: Routledge and Kegan Paul, 1977), 37.

26. Mark Helprin, "Introduction: The Canon Under Siege," in *Best American Short Stories, 1988* (Boston: Houghton Mifflin Company, 1988), xxvii; hereafter cited in the text as Helprin.

27. Anton Chekhov, "Gooseberries," in *"The Wife" and Other Stories*, trans. Constance Garnett (New York: Ecco Press, 1984), 285.

28. William Abrahams, *Prize Stories 1988: The O. Henry Awards* (New York: Anchor Books, Doubleday, 1988), xi.

29. Henri Troyat, *Chekhov*, trans. Michael Henry Heim (New York: E. P. Dutton, 1986), 332.

Part 2

THE WRITER

Introduction

Raymond Carver held definite ideas about writing and was an articulate spokesman on the subject. What comes through in his essays and in the interviews to which he submitted is a self-conscious literary attitude well-suited to the 1980s. His admitted short attention span was shared by an impatient nation. "Get in, get out. Don't linger. Go on."

Such sentiments could have been the credo of a generation. Just as American culture was beginning to demand a return to the basics, Carver's spare kind of story was reaching its zenith. The result was a fortuitous convergence that finally gave him an honored status in American letters, and yet, he remained on intimate terms with the oppressed, inarticulate, and spiritually paralyzed characters he created in his fiction.

The selections included here—"On Writing" and Larry McCaffery and Sinda Gregory's interview with the author—introduce the reader to Carver's attitudes and practices, his stated intentions, the poetics, if you will, that produced the stories. They also capture, I believe, the spirit of a time and a place and the individual who was shaped by that spirit and helped to shape it.

In "On Writing," Carver asserts three principles derived respectively from Ezra Pound, Anton Chekhov, and Geoffrey Wolff: 1) that accuracy of expression is a moral act, 2) that there are consequences in sudden awakenings, and 3) that there is no place in writing for tricks. The last principle of this series, juxtaposed with his confession that talk of innovation makes him nervous, suggests a link between tricks and experimentation, a common attitude of the period and one that says as much about the time and place as it does about Carver.

The McCaffery-Gregory interview, while sustaining that suspicion, reveals a nascent tolerance. We discover an evolution in the writer at the very time he is creating short stories that will testify to a more open approach to innovative fiction. His tribute to Donald Barthelme's vision in the interview is one example of this growth.

In the same space, Carver establishes a relation between autobiographical events and his body of work. Here, also, readers will encounter his acknowledged intentions of investing commonplace objects, events, and expressions with values beyond what their surfaces possess.

What comes through most clearly in these selections is the presence of an individual who is human, with the same misgivings and hesitations most of us suffer, for once again, he affirms that writing was for him an act of discovery. Surprised to learn it was that way for Flannery O'Connor and presumably others, he confesses to a feeling of relief and a sense of being heartened. At the same time, however, we see an individual who is creating short stories in a particular time and place and in so doing helping to recast that period and that landscape.

"On Writing"

Back in the mid-1960s, I found I was having trouble concentrating my attention on long narrative fiction. For a time I experienced difficulty in trying to read it as well as in attempting to write it. My attention span had gone out on me; I no longer had the patience to try to write novels. It's an involved story, too tedious to talk about here. But I know it has much to do now with why I write poems and short stories. Get in, get out. Don't linger. Go on. It could be that I lost any great ambitions at about the same time, in my late twenties. If I did, I think it was good it happened. Ambition and a little luck are good things for a writer to have going for him. Too much ambition and bad luck, or no luck at all, can be killing. There has to be talent.

Some writers have a bunch of talent; I don't know any writers who are without it. But a unique and exact way of looking at things, and finding the right context for expressing that way of looking, that's something else. *The World According to Garp* is, of course, the marvelous world according to John Irving. There is another world according to Flannery O'Connor, and others according to William Faulkner and Ernest Hemingway. There are worlds according to Cheever, Updike, Singer, Stanley Elkin, Ann Beattie, Cynthia Ozick, Donald Barthelme, Mary Robison, William Kittredge, Barry Hannah, Ursula K. Le Guin. Every great or even every very good writer makes the world over according to his own specifications.

It's akin to style, what I'm talking about, but it isn't style alone. It is the writer's particular and unmistakable signature on everything he writes. It is his world and no other. This is one of the things that distinguishes one writer from another. Not talent. There's plenty of that around. But a writer who has some special way of looking at things and who gives artistic expression to that way of looking: that writer may be around for a time.

Isak Dinesen said that she wrote a little every day, without hope and without despair. Someday I'll put that on a three-by-five card and tape

From *Fires*, by Raymond Carver, © 1983. Reprinted by permission of Capra Press, Santa Barbara, California.

it to the wall beside my desk. I have some three-by-five cards on the wall now. "Fundamental accuracy of statement is the ONE sole morality of writing." Ezra Pound. It is not everything by ANY means, but if a writer has "fundamental accuracy of statement" going for him, he's at least on the right track.

I have a three-by-five up there with this fragment of a sentence from a story by Chekov: ". . . and suddenly everything became clear to him." I find these words filled with wonder and possibility. I love their simple clarity, and the hint of revelation that's implied. There is mystery, too. What has been unclear before? Why is it just now becoming clear? What's happened? Most of all—what now? There are consequences as a result of such sudden awakenings. I feel a sharp sense of relief—and anticipation.

I overheard the writer Geoffrey Wolff say "No cheap tricks" to a group of writing students. That should go on a three-by-five card. I'd amend it a little to "No tricks." Period. I hate tricks. At the first sign of a trick or a gimmick in a piece of fiction, a cheap trick or even an elaborate trick, I tend to look for cover. Tricks are ultimately boring, and I get bored easily, which may go along with my not having much of an attention span. But extremely clever chi-chi writing, or just plain tomfoolery writing, puts me to sleep. Writers don't need tricks or gimmicks or even necessarily need to be the smartest fellows on the block. At the risk of appearing foolish, a writer sometimes needs to be able to just stand and gape at this or that thing—a sunset or an old shoe— in absolute and simple amazement.

Some months back, in the *New York Times Book Review*, John Barth said that ten years ago most of the students in his fiction writing seminar were interested in "formal innovation," and this no longer seems to be the case. He's a little worried that writers are going to start writing mom and pop novels in the 1980s. He worries that experimentation may be on the way out, along with liberalism. I get a little nervous if I find myself within earshot of somber discussions about "formal innovation" in fiction writing. Too often "experimentation" is a license to be careless, silly or imitative in the writing. Even worse, a license to try to brutalize or alienate the reader. Too often such writing gives us no news of the world, or else describes a desert landscape and that's all—a few dunes and lizards here and there, but no people; a place uninhabited by anything recognizably human, a place of interest only to a few scientific specialists.

It should be noted that real experiment in fiction is original, hard-earned and cause for rejoicing. But someone else's way of looking at things—Barthelme's, for instance—should not be chased after by other writers. It won't work. There is only one Barthelme, and for another writer to try to appropriate Barthelme's peculiar sensibility or *mise en scene* under the rubric of innovation is for that writer to mess around with chaos and disaster and, worse, self-deception. The real experimenters have to Make It New, as Pound urged, and in the process have to find things out for themselves. But if writers haven't taken leave of their senses, they also want to stay in touch with us, they want to carry news from their world to ours.

It's possible, in a poem or a short story, to write about commonplace things and objects using commonplace but precise language, and to endow those things—a chair, a window curtain, a fork, a stone, a woman's earring—with immense, even startling power. It is possible to write a line of seemingly innocuous dialogue and have it send a chill along the reader's spine—the source of artistic delight, as Nabokov would have it. That's the kind of writing that most interests me. I hate sloppy or haphazard writing whether it flies under the banner of experimentation or else is just clumsily rendered realism. In Isaac Babel's wonderful short story, "Guy de Maupassant," the narrator has this to say about the writing of fiction: "No iron can pierce the heart with such force as a period put just at the right place." This too ought to go on a three-by-five.

Evan Connell said once that he knew he was finished with a short story when he found himself going through it and taking out commas and then going through the story again and putting commas back in the same places. I like that way of working on something. I respect that kind of care for what is being done. That's all we have, finally, the words, and they had better be the right ones, with the punctuation in the right places so that they can best say what they are meant to say. If the words are heavy with the writer's own unbridled emotions, or if they are imprecise and inaccurate for some other reason—if the words are in any way blurred—the reader's eyes will slide right over them and nothing will be achieved. The reader's own artistic sense will simply not be engaged. Henry James called this sort of hapless writing "weak specification."

I have friends who've told me they had to hurry a book because they needed the money, their editor or their wife was leaning on them or leaving them—something, some apology for the writing not being very good. "It would have been better if I'd taken the time." I was dumbfounded when I heard a novelist friend say this. I still am, if I think about it, which I don't. It's none of my business. But if the writing can't be made as good as it is within us to make it, then why do it? In the end, the satisfaction of having done our best, and the proof of that labor, is the one thing we can take into the grave. I wanted to say to my friend, for heaven's sake go do something else. There have to be easier and maybe more honest ways to try and earn a living. Or else just do it to the best of your abilities, your talents, and then don't justify or make excuses. Don't complain, don't explain.

In an essay called, simply enough, "Writing Short Stories," Flannery O'Connor talks about writing as an act of discovery. O'Connor says she most often did not know where she was going when she sat down to work on a short story. She says she doubts that many writers know where they are going when they begin something. She uses "Good Country People" as an example of how she put together a short story whose ending she could not even guess at until she was nearly there:

> When I started writing that story, I didn't know there was going to be a Ph.D. with a wooden leg in it. I merely found myself one morning writing a description of two women I knew something about, and before I realized it, I had equipped one of them with a daughter with a wooden leg. I brought in the Bible salesman, but I had no idea what I was going to do with him. I didn't know he was going to steal that wooden leg until ten or twelve lines before he did it, but when I found out that this was what was going to happen, I realized it was inevitable.

When I read this some years ago it came as a shock that she, or anyone for that matter, wrote stories in this fashion. I thought this was my uncomfortable secret, and I was a little uneasy with it. For sure I thought this way of working on a short story somehow revealed my own shortcomings. I remember being tremendously heartened by reading what she had to say on the subject.

I once sat down to write what turned out to be a pretty good story, though only the first sentence of the story had offered itself to me when I began it. For several days I'd been going around with this sentence in my head: "He was running the vacuum cleaner when the telephone rang." I knew a story was there and that it wanted telling. I felt it in my bones, that a story belonged with that beginning, if I could just have the time to write it. I found the time, an entire day—twelve, fifteen hours even—if I wanted to make use of it. I did, and I sat down in the morning and wrote the first sentence, and other sentences promptly began to attach themselves. I made the story just as I'd make a poem; one line and then the next, and the next. Pretty soon I could see a story, and I knew it was my story, the one I'd been wanting to write.

I like it when there is some feeling of threat or sense of menace in short stories. I think a little menace is fine to have in a story. For one thing, it's good for the circulation. There has to be tension, a sense that something is imminent, that certain things are in relentless motion, or else, most often, there simply won't be a story. What creates tension in a piece of fiction is partly the way the concrete words are linked together to make up the visible action of the story. But it's also the things that are left out, that are implied, the landscape just under the smooth (but sometimes broken and unsettled) surface of things.

V. S. Pritchett's definition of a short story is "something glimpsed from the corner of the eye, in passing." Notice the "glimpse" part of this. First the glimpse. Then the glimpse given life, turned into something that illuminates the moment and may, if we're lucky—that word again—have even further-ranging consequences and meaning. The short story writer's task is to invest the glimpse with all that is in his power. He'll bring his intelligence and literary skill to bear (his talent), his sense of proportion and sense of the fitness of things: of how things out there really are and how he sees those things—like no one else sees them. And this is done through the use of clear and specific language, language used so as to bring to life the details that will light up the story for the reader. For the details to be concrete and convey meaning, the language must be accurate and precisely given. The words can be so precise they may even sound flat, but they can still carry; if used right, they can hit all the notes.

An Interview with Raymond Carver

To be inside a Raymond Carver story is a bit like standing in a model kitchen at Sears—you experience a weird feeling of disjuncture that comes from being in a place where things *appear* to be real and familiar, but where a closer look shows that the turkey is papier-mâché, the broccoli is rubber, and the frilly curtains cover a blank wall. In Carver's fiction things are simply not as they appear. Or, rather, things are *more* than they appear to be, for often commonplace objects—a broken refrigerator, a car, a cigarette, a bottle of beer or whiskey—become transformed in Carver's hands, from realistic props in realistic stories to powerful, emotionally charged signifiers in and of themselves. Language itself undergoes a similar transformation. Since there is little authorial presence and since Carver's characters are often inarticulate and bewildered about the turns their lives have taken, their seemingly banal conversations are typically endowed with unspoken intensity and meaning. Watching Carver's characters interact, then, is rather like spending an evening with two close friends who you know have had a big fight just before you arrived: even the most ordinary gestures and exchanges have transformed meanings, hidden tensions, emotional depths.

Although Carver published two books of poetry in the late 1960s and early '70s (*Near Klamath* in 1968 and *Winter Insomnia* in 1970), it was his book of stories, *Will You Please Be Quiet, Please?*, published in 1976 and nominated for the National Book Award, that established his national reputation as a writer with a unique voice and style. Pared down, stark, yet intense, these stories can perhaps best be compared in their achievement to a work outside literature, Bruce Springsteen's album *Nebraska*. Like Springsteen, Carver writes about troubled people on the outs—out of work, out of love, out of touch—whose confusion, turmoils, and poignancy are conveyed through an interplay of surface

From *Alive and Writing: Interviews with American Authors of the 1980s*, conducted and edited by Larry McCaffery and Sinda Gregory, 1987. Reprinted by permission of University of Illinois Press. © 1987 by the Board of Trustees of the University of Illinois.

details. His next collection, *What We Talk About When We Talk About Love* (1981), takes this elliptical, spare style even further. With just enough description to set the scene, just enough interpretation of motivation to clarify the action, these stories offer the illusion of the authorless story in which "reality" is transcribed and meaning arises without mediation. This move toward greater and greater economy was abandoned by Carver in *Cathedral* (1983); as the following conversation indicates, changes in his personal life affected his aesthetics. While still written in his distinctive voice, these stories explore more interior territory using less constricted language.

This change (mirrored as well in his most recent collection of poems, *Ultramarine* [1986]) is apparent not just in style but in the themes found in *Cathedral*, which contains several stories of hope and spiritual communion. As we drove to Carver's home outside Port Angeles, Washington, we were still formulating questions designed to reveal why *Cathedral* was less bleak, less constricted. But nothing very devious or complex was required. Sitting in his living room, which offers an amazing vista of the blustery Strait of Juan de Fuca, Carver was obviously a happy man—happy in the homelife he shares with Tess Gallagher, his work, his victory over alcohol, and his new direction. Replying to our questions in a soft, low voice with the same kind of direct honesty evident in his fiction, Carver seemed less like an author of three collections of stories; a book of essays, short stories, and poems (*Fires*, 1983); and three volumes of poetry than he did a writer starting out, eager to begin work, anxious to see where his life would lead.

Larry McCaffery: In an essay in *Fires* you say, "To write a novel, a writer should be living in a world that makes sense, a world that the writer can believe in, draw a bead on, and then write about accurately. A world that will, for a time anyway, stay fixed in one place. Along with this there has to be a belief in the essential *correctness* of that world." Am I right in assuming that you've arrived at a place, physically and psychologically, where you can believe in the "correctness" of your world enough to sustain a novel-length imaginary world?

Raymond Carver: I do feel I've arrived at such a place. My life is very different now than it used to be; it seems much more comprehensible to me. It was previously almost impossible for me to imagine trying to write a novel in the state of incomprehension, despair, really, that I was in. I have hope now, and I didn't have hope then—"hope" in the sense of belief. I believe now that the world will exist for me tomorrow in the same way it exists for me today. That didn't used to be the case. For a long time I found myself living by the seat of my pants, making things terribly difficult for myself and everyone around me by my drinking. In this second life, this post-drinking life, I still retain a certain sense of pessimism, I suppose, but I also have belief in and love for the things of this world. Needless to say, I'm not talking about microwave ovens, jet planes, and expensive cars.

LM: Does this mean you have plans to try your hand at a novel?

RC: Yes. Maybe. Maybe after I finish this new manuscript of poems. Maybe then I'll return to fiction and do some longer fiction, a novel or a novella. I feel like I'm reaching the end of the time of writing poetry. In another month or so I'll have written something like 150–180 poems during this period, so I feel like I'm about to run out this string, and then I can go back to fiction. It's important to me, though, to have this new book of poems in manuscript in the cupboard. When *Cathedral* came out, that cupboard was absolutely bare; I don't want something like that to happen again. Tobias Wolff recently finished a book of stories that he turned in to Houghton Mifflin; he asked me if it was hard for me to start work again after finishing a book, because he was having a hard time getting going again. I told him not to worry about it *now*, but that he should make sure he's well along on something by the time his book is ready to come out. If you've emptied all your cupboards, the way I had after *Cathedral*, it can be difficult to catch your stride again.

Sinda Gregory: Your newfound "belief in and love for the things of this world" is very evident in some of the stories in *Cathedral*, especially in the title story.

RC: That story was very much an "opening up" process for me—I mean that in every sense. "Cathedral" *was* a larger, grander story than anything I had previously written. When I began writing that story I felt that I was breaking out of something I had put myself into, both personally and aesthetically. I simply couldn't go on any farther in the direction I had been going in *What We Talk About When We Talk About Love*. Oh, I *could* have, I suppose, but I didn't want to. Some of the stories were becoming too attenuated. I didn't write anything for five or six months after that book came out. I literally wrote nothing except letters. So it was especially pleasing to me that, when I finally sat down to write again, I wrote *that* story, "Cathedral." It felt like I had never written anything that way before. I could let myself *go* in some way, I didn't have to impose the restrictions on myself that I had in the earlier stories. The last story I wrote for the collection was "Fever," which was also just about the longest story I've ever written. And it's affirmative, I think, positive in its outlook. Really, the whole collection is different, and the next book is going to be different as well!

LM: What does it mean to a writer like you to find yourself, relatively suddenly, in such a different frame of mind? Do you find it difficult today to write about the despair, emotional turmoil, and hopelessness that is so much a part of the vision of your earlier fiction?

RC: No, because when I need to open this door to my imagination—stare out over the window casement, what Keats called his "magic casements"—I can remember exactly the texture of that despair and hopelessness, I can still taste it, feel it. The things that are emotionally meaningful to me are still very much alive and available to me, even though the circumstances of my personal life have changed. Merely because my physical surroundings and my mental state are different today doesn't mean, of course, that I still don't know exactly what I was talking about in the earlier stories. I can bring all that back if I choose to, but I'm finding that I am not driven to write about it exclusively. That's not to say I'm interested in writing about life here, where I live in Four Seasons Ranch, this chichi development. If you look carefully at *Cathedral*, you'll find that many of those stories have to do with that other life, which is still very much with me. But not all of them do, which is why the book feels different to me.

LM: A striking example of the differences you're referring to can be seen when you compare "A Small Good Thing" (in *Cathedral*) with the earlier version, "The Bath," which appeared in *What We Talk About*. The differences between the two versions are clearly fundamental.

RC: Certainly there's a lot more optimism in "A Small Good Thing." In my own mind I consider them to be really two entirely different stories, not just different versions of the same story; it's hard to even look on them as coming from the same source. I went back to that one, as well as several others, because I felt there was unfinished business that needed attending to. The story hadn't been told originally; it had been messed around with, condensed and compressed in "The Bath" to highlight the qualities of menace that I wanted to emphasize—you see this with the business about the baker, the phone call, with its menacing voice on the other line, the bath, and so on. But I still felt there was unfinished business, so in the midst of writing these other stories for *Cathedral* I went back to "The Bath" and tried to see what aspects of it needed to be enhanced, redrawn, reimagined.

When I was done, I was amazed because it seemed so much better. I've had people tell me that they much prefer "The Bath," which is fine, but "A Small Good Thing" seems to me to be a better story.

SG: Many of your stories either open with the ordinary being slightly disturbed by this sense of menace you've just mentioned or develop in that direction. Is this tendency the result of your conviction that the world *is* menacing for most people? Or does it have more to do with an aesthetic choice—that menace contains more interesting possibilities for storytelling?

RC: The world is a menacing place for many of the people in my stories, yes. The people I've chosen to write about *do* feel menace, and I think many, if not most, people feel the world is a menacing place. Probably not so many people who will see this interview feel menace in the sense I'm talking about. Most of our friends and acquaintances, yours and mine, don't feel this way. But try living on the other side of the tracks for a while. Menace is there, and it's palpable. As to the second part of your question, that's true, too. Menace does contain, for me at least, more interesting possibilities to explore.

SG: When you look back at your stories, do you find "unfinished business" in most of them?

RC: This may have to do with newfound confidence, but I feel that the stories in *Cathedral* are *finished* in a way I rarely felt about my stories previously. I've never even read the book since I saw it in bound galleys. I was happy about those stories, not worried about them; I felt there was simply no need to mess around with them, make new judgments about them. A lot of this surely has to do with this whole complicated business about the new circumstances in my life, my sense of confidence in what I'm doing with my life and my work. For such a long time, when I was an alcoholic, I was very *un*-confident and had such very low self-esteem, both as a person and as a writer, that I was always questioning my judgments about everything. Every good thing that has happened to me during the last several years has been an incentive to do more and do better. I know I've felt that recently in writing all these poems, and it's affecting my fiction as well. I'm more sure of my voice, more sure of *something*. I felt a bit tentative when I started writing those poems, maybe partly because I hadn't written any for so long, but I soon found a voice—and that voice gave me confidence. Now when I start writing something, I mean *now* in these last few years, I don't have that sense of fooling around, of being tentative, of not knowing what to do, of having to sharpen a lot of pencils. When

I go to my desk now and pick up a pen, I really know what I have to do. It's a totally different feeling.

SG: What was it that made you return to poetry after all those years of focusing exclusively on fiction?

RC: I came out here to Port Angeles with the intention of bringing to completion a long piece of fiction I had started back at Syracuse. But when I got out here, I sat around for five days or so, just enjoying the peace and quiet (I didn't have a television or radio), a welcome change from all the distractions going on at Syracuse. After those five days I found myself reading a little poetry. Then one night I sat down and wrote a poem. I hadn't written any poetry in two years or more, and somewhere in the back of my mind I was lamenting the fact that I hadn't written any—or really even given any serious thought to poetry writing for a long time. During the period when I was writing the stories that went into *Cathedral*, for example, I was feeling I couldn't have written a poem if someone had put a gun to my head. I wasn't even *reading* any poetry, except for Tess's. At any rate, I wrote this first poem that night, and then the next day I got up and wrote another poem. The day after that I wrote *another* poem. This went on for ten straight weeks; the poems seemed to be coming out of this wonderful rush of energy. At night I'd feel totally empty, absolutely whipped out, and I'd wonder if anything would be left the next morning. But the next day there *was* something—the well hadn't gone dry. So I'd get up, drink coffee, and go to my desk and write another poem. When it was happening I felt almost as if I were being given a good shaking, and suddenly my keys were falling out of my pockets. I've never had a period in which I've taken such joy in the act of writing as I did in those two months.

LM: You've said that it no longer matters where you are living as far as your writing is concerned. Has that feeling changed?

RC: I'd certainly retract that statement nowadays. Having this place here in Port Angeles has been very important to me, and I'm sure coming out here helped me get started writing poetry. I think it was getting clear away from the outdoors and my contact with nature that made me feel I was losing whatever it was that made me want to write poetry. I had spent the summer of 1982 out here (not in this house, but in a little cabin a few miles from here), and I wrote four stories in a fairly short period of time, although they took place indoors and didn't have anything specifically to do with this locale. But without question my poetry came back to me because of this relocation. It had been increasingly difficult for me to work in Syracuse, which is why I pulled up stakes and came out here. There was just too much going on back in Syracuse, especially after *Cathedral* came out and there was so much happening in connection with the book. There were people coming in and out of the house, and a lot of other business that never seemed to end. The telephone was ringing all the time, and Tess was teaching, and there were a certain number of social obligations. This might only mean having an occasional dinner with dear friends, whom it was always a pleasure to see, but all this was taking me away from my work. It got to the point where even hearing the cleaning woman, hearing her make the bed or vacuum the rug or wash the dishes, bothered me. So I came out here, and when Tess left to go back to Syracuse on September 1, I stayed on for another four weeks to write and fish. I did a lot of work during those weeks, and when I got back to Syracuse I thought I could keep up that rhythm. I did manage to for a few days, but then I found myself limited to editing the stuff I had written out here. Finally, the last few weeks or so, it was all I could do to make it from day to day. I would consider it a good day if I could take care of my correspondence. That's a hell of a situation for a writer to be in. I wasn't sorry to leave, even though I have some dear friends there.

SG: In the *Esquire* article you wrote about your father, you mention a poem you wrote, "Photograph of My Father in His 22nd Year," and comment that "the poem was a way of trying to connect up with him." Does poetry offer you a more direct way of connecting to your past?

RC: I'd say it does. It's a more immediate way, a faster means of connecting. Doing these poems satisfies my desire to write something, and tell a story, every day—sometimes two or three times a day, even four or five times a day. But in regard to connecting up to my past, it must be said of my poems (and my stories, too) that even though they may all have some basis in my experience, they are also *imaginative*. They're totally made up, most of them.

LM: So even in your poetry that persona who is speaking is never precisely "you"?

RC: No. Same as in my stories, those stories told in the first person, for instance. Those "I" narrators aren't me.

SG: In your poem "For Smera, with Martial Vigor," your narrator says to a woman, "All poems are love poems." Is this true in some sense of your own poetry?

RC: Every poem is act of love, and faith. There is so little other reward for writing poems, either monetarily or in terms of, you know, fame and glory, that the act of writing a poem has to be an act that justifies itself and really has no other end in sight. To *want* to do it, you really have to love doing it. In that sense, then, every poem *is* a "love poem."

LM: Have you found it a problem to move back and forth between genres? Is a different composition process involved?

RC: The juggling has never seemed a problem. I suppose it would have been more unusual in a writer who hadn't worked in both areas to the extent that I have. Actually I've always felt and maintained that the poem is closer in its effect and in the way it is composed to a short story than the short story is to a novel. Stories and poems have more in common in what the writing is aiming for, in the compression of language and emotion, and in the care and control required to achieve their effects. To me, the process of writing a story or a poem has never seemed very different. Everything I write comes from the same spring, or source, whether it's a story or an essay or a poem or a screenplay. When I sit down to write, I literally start with a sentence or a line. I always have to have that first line in my head, whether it's a poem or a story. Later on everything else is subject to change, but that first line rarely changes. Somehow it shoves me on to the second line, and then the process begins to take on momentum and acquire a direction. Nearly everything I write goes through many revisions, and I do a lot of backing up, to-and-froing. I don't mind revising; I actually enjoy it, in fact. Don Hall has taken seven years to write and polish the poems that make up his new book. He's revised some of the poems a hundred and fifty times or so. I'm not *that* obsessive, but I do a lot of revising, it's true. And I think friends of mine are a bit dubious about how my poems are going to turn out. They just don't think poems can or should be written as fast as I wrote these. I'll just have to show them.

LM: One possible source of interaction between your poetry and fiction has to do with the way the impact of your stories often seems to center on a single image: a peacock, a cigarette, a car. These images seem to function like poetic images—that is, they organize the story, draw our responses into a complex set of associations. How conscious are you of developing this kind of controlling image?

RC: I'm not consciously creating a central image in my fiction that would control a story the way images, or an image, often control a work of poetry. I have an image in my head but it seems to emerge out of the story in an organic, natural fashion. For instance, I didn't realize in advance that the peacock image would so dominate "Feathers." The peacock just seemed like something a family who lived in the country on a small farm might have running around the house. It *wasn't* something I placed there in an effort to have it perform as a symbol. When I'm writing I don't think in terms of developing symbols or of what an image will do. When I hit on an image that seems to be working and it stands for what it is supposed to stand for (it may stand for several other things as well), that's great. But I don't think of them self-consciously. They seem to evolve, occur. I truly invent them and *then* certain things seem to form around them as events occur, recollection and imagination begin to color them, and so forth.

SG: In an essay in *Fires*, you make a remark that perfectly describes for me one of the most distinctive things about your fiction: "It's possible, in a poem or a short story, to write about commonplace things and objects using commonplace language and to endow those things— a chair, a window curtain, a fork, a stone, a woman's earring—with immense, even startling power." I realize that every story is different in this regard, but how *does* one go about investing these ordinary objects with such power and emphasis?

RC: I'm not given to rhetoric or abstraction in my life, my thinking, or my writing, so when I write about people I want them to be placed within a setting that must be made as palpable as possible. This might mean including as part of the setting a television or a table or a felt-tipped pen lying on a desk, but if these things are going to be introduced into the scene at all, they shouldn't be inert. I don't mean that they should take on a life of their own, precisely, but they should make their presence *felt* in some way. If you are going to describe a spoon or a chair or a TV set, you don't want simply to set these things into the scene and let them go. You want to give them some weight, connecting these things to the lives around them. I see these objects as playing a role in the stories; they're not "characters" in the sense that the people are, but they are *there* and I want my readers to be aware that they're there, to know that this ashtray is here, that the TV is there (and that it's going or it's not going), that the fireplace has old pop cans in it.

SG: What appeals to you about writing stories and poems, rather than longer forms?

RC: For one thing, whenever I pick up a literary magazine, the first thing I look at is the poetry, and then I'll read the stories. I hardly ever read anything else, the essays, reviews, what have you. So I suppose I was drawn to the *form*, and I mean the brevity, of both poetry and short fiction from the beginning. Also, poetry and short fiction seemed to be things I could get done in a reasonable period of time. When I started out as a writer, I was moving around a lot, and there were daily distractions, weird jobs, family responsibilities. My life seemed very fragile, so I wanted to be able to start something that I felt I had a reasonable chance of seeing through to a finish—which meant I needed to finish things in a hurry, a short period of time. As I just mentioned, poetry and fiction seemed so close to one another in form and intent, so close to what I was interested in doing, that early on I didn't have any trouble moving back and forth between them.

LM: Who were the poets you were reading and admiring, perhaps being influenced by, when you were developing your notions of the craft of poetry? Your outdoor settings may suggest James Dickey, but a more likely influence seems to me to be William Carlos Williams.

RC: Williams was indeed a big influence; he was my greatest hero. When I started out writing poetry I was reading his poems. Once I even had the temerity to write him and ask for a poem for a little magazine I was starting at Chico State University called *Selection.* I think we put out three issues; I edited the first issue. But William Carlos Williams actually sent me a poem. I was thrilled and surprised to see his signature under the poem. That's an understatement. Dickey's poetry did not mean so much, even though he was just coming into his full powers at about the time when I was starting out in the early '60s. I liked Creeley's poetry, and later Robert Bly, Don Hall, Galway Kinnell, James Wright, Dick Hugo, Gary Snyder, Archie Ammons, Merwin, Ted Hughes. I really didn't know anything when I was starting out, I just sort of read what people gave me, but I've never been drawn to highly intellectualized poetry—the metaphysical poets or whatever.

LM: Is abstraction or intellectualism something that usually turns you off in a work?

RC: I don't think it's an anti-intellectual bias, if that's what you mean. There are just some works that I can respond to and others operating at levels I don't connect with. I suppose I'm not interested in what you might call the "well-made poem," for example. When I see one I'm tempted to react by saying, "Oh, that's just poetry." I'm looking for something else, something that's *not just* a good poem. Practically any good graduate student in a creative writing program can write a good poem. I'm looking for something beyond that. Maybe something rougher.

SG: A reader is immediately struck with the "pared down" quality

of your work, especially your work before *Cathedral*. Was this style
something that evolved, or had it been with you from the beginning?

RC: From the very beginning I loved the rewriting process as much
as the initial execution. I've always loved taking sentences and playing
with them, rewriting them, paring them down to where they seem
solid somehow. This may have resulted from being John Gardner's student, because he told me something I immediately responded to: If
you can say it in fifteen words rather than twenty or thirty words, then
say it in fifteen words. That struck me with the force of revelation.
There I was, groping to find my own way, and here someone was telling me something that somehow conjoined with what I already wanted
to do. It was the most natural thing in the world for me to go back and
refine what was happening on the page and eliminate the padding.
The last few days I've been reading Flaubert's letters, and he says
some things that seem relevant to my own aesthetic. At one point when
Flaubert was writing *Madame Bovary*, he would knock off at midnight
or one in the morning and write letters to his mistress, Louise Colet,
about the construction of the book and his general notion of aesthetics.
One passage he wrote her that really struck me was when he said, "The
artist in his work must be like God in his creation—invisible and all
powerful; he must be everywhere felt but nowhere seen." I like the
last part of that especially. There's another interesting remark when
Flaubert is writing to his editors at the magazine that published the
book in installments. They were just getting ready to serialize *Madame
Bovary* and were going to make a lot of cuts in the text because they
were afraid they were going to be closed down by the government if
they published it just as Flaubert wrote it, so Flaubert tells them that
if they make the cuts they can't publish the book, but they'll still be
friends. The last line of this letter is: "I know how to distinguish between literature and literary business"—another insight I respond to.
Even in these letters his prose is astonishing: "Prose must stand up-
right from one end to the other, like a wall whose ornamentation continues down to its very base." "Prose is architecture." "Everything
must be done coldly, with poise." "Last week I spent five days writing
one page." One of the interesting things about the Flaubert book is
the way it demonstrates how self-consciously he was setting out to do
something very special and different with prose. He consciously tried
to make prose an art form. If you look at what else was being published
in Europe in 1855, when *Madame Bovary* was published, you realize
what an achievement the book really is.

LM: In addition to John Gardner, were there other writers who affected your fictional sensibility early on? Hemingway comes immediately to mind.

RC: Hemingway was certainly an influence. I didn't read him until I was in college and then I read the wrong book (*Across the River and into the Trees*) and didn't like him very much. But a little later I read *In Our Time* in a class and I found that he was marvelous. I remember thinking, This is *it;* if you can write prose like this, you've done something.

LM: In your essays you've spoken out against literary tricks or gimmicks—yet I would argue that your own works are really experimental in the same sense that Hemingway's fiction was. What's the difference between literary experimentalism that seems legitimate to you and the kind that isn't?

RC: I'm against tricks that call attention to themselves in an effort to be clever or merely devious. I read a review this morning in *Publishers Weekly* of a novel that is coming out next spring; the book sounded so disjointed and filled with things that have nothing to do with life, or literature as I know it, that I felt certain I wouldn't read it except under pain of death. A writer mustn't lose sight of the story. I'm not interested in works that are all texture and no flesh and blood. I guess I'm old fashioned enough to feel that the reader must somehow be involved at the human level. And that there is still, or ought to be, a compact between writer and reader. Writing, or any form of artistic endeavor, is not just expression, it's communication. When a writer stops being truly interested in communicating something and is only aiming at expressing something, and that not very well—well, they can express themselves by going out to the streetcorner and hollering. A short story or a novel or a poem should deliver a certain number of emotional punches. You can judge that work by how strong these punches are and how many are thrown. If it's all just a bunch of head trips or games, I'm not interested. Work like that is just chaff: it'll blow away with the first good wind.

LM: Are there out-and-out experimentalists whom you *do* admire? I was wondering about your reaction to Donald Barthelme's work, for example.

RC: I like his work. I didn't care much for it when I first started reading it. It seemed so strange that I stopped reading him for a while. Also, he was, or so it seemed to me, the generation right ahead of mine, and it wouldn't do at the time to like it all that much! But then

I read *Sixty Stories* a couple of years ago. He's terrific! I found that the more I read his stories, the more regard I began to have for them. Barthelme has done a *world* of work, he's a true innovator who's not being devious or stupid or mean spirited or experimenting for experimenting's sake. He's uneven, but then who isn't? Certainly his effect on creative writing classes has been tremendous (as they say, he's often imitated but never duplicated). He's like Allen Ginsberg in that he opened a gate, and afterward a great flood of work by other people poured through, some of it good and a lot of it awful. I'm not worried that all that bad stuff which has followed after Barthelme or Ginsberg will push the good stuff off the shelves. It will just disappear on its own.

SG: One of the nontraditional aspects of your own fiction is that your stories don't tend to have the "shape" of the classically rendered story: the introduction/conflict/development/resolution structure of so much fiction. Instead there is often a static or ambiguous, open-ended quality to your stories. I assume you feel that the experiences you are describing simply don't lend themselves to being rendered within the familiar framework.

RC: It would be inappropriate, and to a degree impossible, to resolve things neatly for these people and situations I'm writing about. It's probably typical for writers to admire other writers who are their opposites in terms of intentions and effects, and I'll admit that I greatly admire stories that unfold in that classic mode, with conflict, resolution, and denouement. But even though I can respect those stories, and sometimes even be a little envious, I can't write them. The writer's job, if he or she has a job, is not to provide conclusions or answers. If the story answers *itself*, its problems and conflicts, and meets its *own* requirements, then that's enough. On the other hand, I want to make certain my readers aren't left feeling cheated in one way or another when they've finished my stories. It's important for writers to provide enough to satisfy readers, even if they don't provide "the" answers, or clear resolutions.

LM: Another distinctive feature of your work is that you usually present characters that most writers don't deal with—that is, people who are basically inarticulate, who can't verbalize their plights, who often don't seem to really grasp what is happening to them.

RC: I don't think of this as being especially "distinctive" or nontraditional because I feel perfectly comfortable with these people while I'm working. I've known people like this all my life. Essentially, I *am* one of those confused, befuddled people, I come from people like that, those are the people I've worked with and earned my living beside for years. That's why I've never had any interest whatsoever in writing a story or a poem that has anything to do with the academic life, with teachers or students and so forth. I'm just not that interested. The things that have made an indelible impression on me are the things I saw in lives I witnessed being lived around me, and in the life I myself lived. These were lives where people really *were* scared when someone knocked on their door, day or night, or when the telephone rang; they didn't know how they were going to pay the rent or what they could do if their refrigerator went out. Anatole Broyard tries to criticize my story "Preservation" by saying, "So the refrigerator breaks—why don't they just call a repairman and get it fixed?" That kind of remark is dumb. You bring a repairman out to fix your refrigerator and it's sixty bucks to *fix* it; and who knows how much if the thing is completely broken? Well, Broyard may not be aware of it, but some people can't afford to bring in a repairman if it's going to cost them sixty bucks, just like they don't get to a doctor if they don't have insurance, and their teeth go bad because they can't afford to go to a dentist when they need one. That kind of situation doesn't seem unrealistic or artificial to me. It also doesn't seem that, in focusing on this group of people, I have really been doing anything all that different from other writers. Chekhov was writing about a submerged population a hundred years ago. Short story writers have always been doing that. Not all of Chekhov's stories are about people who are down and out, but a significant number of them deal with that submerged population I'm talking about. He wrote about doctors and businessmen and teachers sometimes, but he also gave voice to people who were not so articulate. He found a means of letting those people have their say as well. So in writing about people who aren't so articulate and who are confused and scared, I'm not doing anything radically different.

LM: Aren't there formal problems in writing about this group of people? I mean, you can't have them sit around in drawing rooms endlessly analyzing their situations, the way James does, or, in a different sense, the way Bellow does. I suppose setting the scene, composing it, must be especially important from a technical standpoint.

RC: If you mean literally just setting the scene, that's the least of my worries. The scene is easy to set: I just open the door and see what's inside. I pay a lot of attention to trying to make the people talk the right way. By this I don't mean just *what* they say, but *how* they say it, and *why*. I guess *tone* is what I'm talking about, partly. There's never any chit-chat in my stories. Everything said is for a reason and adds, I want to think, to the overall impression of the story.

SG: People usually emphasize the realistic aspect of your work, but I feel there's a quality about your fiction that is *not* basically realistic. It's as if something is happening almost off the page, a dreamy sense of irrationality, almost like Kafka's fiction.

RC: Presumably my fiction is in the realistic tradition (as opposed to the really far-out side), but just telling it like it is bores me. It really does. People couldn't possibly read pages of description about the way people *really* talk, about what *really* happens in their lives. They'd just snore away, of course. If you look carefully at my stories, I don't think you'll find people talking the way people do in real life. People always say that Hemingway had a great ear for dialogue, and he did. But no one ever talked in real life like they do in Hemingway's fiction. At least not until after they've *read* Hemingway.

LM: In "Fires," you say that it is not true for you, as it was with Flannery O'Connor or Gabriel García Márquez, that most of the stuff that has gone into your fiction had already happened to you before you were twenty. You go on to say, "Most of what now strikes me as story 'material' presented itself to me after I was twenty. I really don't remember much about my life before I became a parent. I really don't feel that anything happened in my life until I was twenty and married and had kids." Would you still agree with that statement? I say this because we were both struck, after we read the piece about your father in *Esquire*, with how much your description of your childhood and relationship with your father seemed relevant to your fictional world in various ways.

RC: That statement certainly felt true when I wrote it—it simply didn't seem that much had truly happened to me until I became a father, at least the sorts of things I could (or wanted to) transform in my stories. But I was also just gaining some perspective on various aspects of my life when I wrote "Fires," and by the time I wrote the piece on my father for *Esquire* I had even more perspective on things. But I see what you're saying. I had touched on something in a very close way in regard to my father when I wrote that essay, which I wrote very quickly and which seemed to come to me very directly. I still feel, though, that the piece on my father is an exception. In that instance I could go back and touch some "source material" from my early life, but that life exists for me as through a scrim of rain.

SG: What kind of a kid were you in that earlier life?

112

RC: A dreamy kid. I wanted to be a writer and I mostly followed my nose as far as reading was concerned. I'd go to the library and check out books on the Spanish conquistadors, or historical novels, whatever struck my fancy, books on shipbuilding, anything that caught my eye. I didn't have any instruction in that regard at all; I'd just go down to the library once a week and browse. All in all, I'd say my childhood was fairly conventional in many respects. We were a poor family, didn't have a car for the longest while, but I didn't miss not having a car. My parents worked and struggled and finally became what I guess you'd call lower middle class. But for the longest while we didn't have much of anything in the way of material goods, or spiritual goods or values either. But I didn't have to go out and work in the fields when I was ten years old or anything of that sort. Mainly I just wanted to fish and hunt and ride around in cars with other guys. Date girls. Things like that. I sponged off my folks as long as I could. The pickings were slim at times, but they bought me things. They even bought me my cigarettes the first year or two I was smoking; I didn't have a job and I guess they knew I would have gone out and stolen them if they didn't buy them for me. But I did want to write, which might have been the only thing that set me apart from my friends. There was one other kid in high school who was my friend and who wanted to write, so we would talk about books. But that was about it. An undistinguished childhood.

SG: Was your father much of a storyteller?

RC: He read to me a little when I was a kid. Mainly Zane Grey stories that he'd read when I'd ask him to (he had a few of those books in the house). But he also told me stories.

LM: You've referred to the bad times you went through with your drinking in the '60s and '70s. In retrospect, was there anything positive at all that came out of those experiences?

RC: Obviously my drinking experiences helped me write several stories that have to do with alcoholism. But the fact that I went through that and was able to write those stories was nothing short of a miracle. No, I don't see anything coming out of my drinking experiences except waste and pain and misery. And it was that way for everybody involved in my life. No good came out of it except in the way that someone might spend ten years in the penitentiary and then come out of that and write about the experience. Despite that comical remark Richard Nixon made about writing and prison at the time when he was about to be impeached, you have to take it on faith that prison life is not the best for a writer.

LM: So you never used any of those confessional stories that one hears at AA meetings as the starting point for one of your stories?

RC: No, I never have. I've heard a lot of stories in AA but most of them I forgot immediately. Oh, I recall a few, but none of them ever struck me as material I wanted to use for a story. Certainly I never went to those meetings thinking of them as possible source materials for my work. To the extent that my stories have to do with drinking, they all pretty much have some starting point in my own experience rather than in the funny, crazy, sad stories I heard at AA. Right now I feel there are enough drinking stories in my work, so I'm not interested in writing them anymore. Not that I have a quota in the back of my mind for any particular type of story, but I'm ready to move on to something else.

SG: I wonder if you're ready to move on to writing more about the outdoors or nature once again. Those elements seem to be missing from your recent work.

RC: I began writing by wanting to write about those things like hunting and fishing that played a real part in my emotional life. And I did write about nature quite a lot in my early poems and stories: you can find it in many of the stories in *Furious Seasons* and in some of the ones in *Will You Please Be Quiet, Please?* and in a lot of the poems. Then I seemed to lose that contact with nature, so I haven't set many of my recent stories in the outdoors—although I suspect I will in the time to come, since a lot of the poems I've recently been writing are set outside. The water has been coming into these poems, and the moon, and the mountains and the sky. I'm sure this will make a lot of people in Manhattan laugh! Talk of tides and the trees, whether the fish are biting or not biting. These things are going to work their way back into my fiction. I feel directly in touch with my surroundings now in a way I haven't felt in years. It just so happened that this was channeled into what I was writing at the time, which was poetry. If I had started a novel or some stories, this contact I've reestablished would have emerged there as well.

SG: Who are the contemporary writers you admire or feel some affinity with?

RC: There are many. I just finished Edna O'Brien's selected stories, *A Fanatic Heart*. She's wonderful. And Tobias Wolff, Bobbie Ann Mason, Ann Beattie, Joy Williams, Richard Ford, Ellen Gilchrist, Bill Kittredge, Alice Munro, Frederick Barthelme. Barry Hannah's short stories. Joyce Carol Oates and John Updike. So many others. It's a fine time to be alive, and writing.

Part 3

THE CRITICS

Introduction

At the end of my preface to this book, I urge readers to keep in mind that critical value lies not in any single answer to questions of meaning, but in the questioning itself. In keeping with that spirit of open inquiry and in the hope of encouraging readers to develop their own original analyses, I include here excellent criticism that exposes the reader to different approaches to Carver's fiction and often reaches conclusions quite different from my own.

Kathleen Westfall Shute's "Finding the Words: The Struggle for Salvation in the Fiction of Raymond Carver" stresses Carver's treatment of redemption and Eucharistic iconography in "A Small, Good Thing" and the contemporary, but symbolic parallel with events following the Passion in "So Much Water So Close to Home." Like Carver, who acknowledged some critics preferred "The Bath" to "A Small, Good Thing," Westfall Shute is aware of the accusations of sentimentality in the later story. For her, such claims miss the point because there still remains no automatic, clear road to salvation. Victories are still relative, possibly even Pyrrhic.

In "Raymond Carver and the Menace of Minimalism," Mark Facknitz finds the reductive and allusive techniques of minimalism everywhere in our culture, in the popular forms of television and in commonplace cinematic devices. He sees this result, not so much as a matter of craft, but as a problem of vision. He argues that in all of Carver's work, including the new pieces of *Where I'm Calling From*, there are stories in which only the most devoted and charitable reader can find mythic or archetypal traces.

However, when Carver moves in the representative late stories from the menace of a minimalist worldview to the world itself, the stories function as tragic allegories. Minimalism itself represents the nothingness that threatens the implied reader, the nameless narrator, and the harried protagonist alike.

Adam Meyer's "Now You See Him, Now You Don't, Now You Do Again: The Evolution of Raymond Carver's Minimalism" traces what I have called the form of Carver's body of fiction, comparing it to the shape of an hourglass in order to make a lifetime of work immediately visible to all readers. With sharp analysis and a wealth of documentation, Meyer outlines Carver's evolution from a comparatively wide perception and style in the earliest fiction through the straitened contours of *What We Talk about When We Talk about Love* to the opening up again of the late fiction.

Kathleen Westfall Shute

In his earlier stories, Raymond Carver's characters seemed unlikely candidates for a philosophical quest into meaning. Hospital orderlies, mill-hands, janitors, hawkers of vitamins and vacuums door-to-door, they were ordinary to a fault. Underperceptive and often despairing, they sweated out their lives in what Carver has called "the crap jobs"— those who were lucky enough to have had work at all. From the earliest moments of childhood, they fell victim to a trap-line of societal and self-made snares. They married young, too young. The lust that was mistaken for love usually disintegrated amid the onslaught of children, dirty laundry, and "making it" month-to-month. Invariably, things fell apart. Alliances dissolved in this bleak, existentialist universe, as did eventually even the semblance of order. The fridge squirted its suicidal pool of refrigerant to the floor just as the final notice came about the color tv. Carver's folk were bankrupted, pink-slipped, often left to stumble alone through a detritus that was at core artificial and peculiarly American.

To be sure, there was in Carver's minimalistic world "relief" of a sort: in drink, in drugs, in promiscuity. His protagonists could try running, firing up their rattletrap cars to skip town to some "better"—and thoroughly undefinable—place. More ominously, when the palpable menace that is ubiquitous in Carver's low-rent landscape came too close, when the tension churned too furiously, characters sometimes exploded, beating, even killing, each other. But the release such action brought was, from the first, fraudulent. Though the sharp edges Carver had created might be blunted temporarily by such tactics, they retained their ability to cut. Time and again, his characters discovered this. Bleeding, they were pressed for some resolution, some response of their own by story's close. Often, we found them shrugging. Muddled and immobilized, they seemed incapable of even an attempt to save themselves. Worse—and emblematic perhaps of a greater despair, a cultural hopelessness—they seemed reduced to the level of static mannequins, deaf to and mute about their situations, the cat (or Carver's own tragic *ennui*) having irrevocably caught them by the tongue.

While this is clearly the harsh paradigm established in Carver's first three volumes of short fiction (*Will You Please Be Quiet, Please?*, 1976; *Furious Seasons*, 1977; and *What We Talk About When We Talk About Love*,

From "Finding the Words: The Struggle for Salvation in the Fiction of Raymond Carver," *Hollins Critic*, 24 no. 5 (1987): 1–9. © 1987 the *Hollins Critic*. Reprinted by permission. The documentation has been altered to conform with that of this book.

1981), the pattern recently appears to be changing. In *Fires: Essays, Poems, Stories, 1966–1982* (1983) and *Cathedral* (1984), nominated for both a National Book Critics Circle Award and a Pulitzer, Carver, for reasons he has largely attributed to his recovery from alcoholism, has begun to afford his characters the gift he has always granted the reader: some light by which to navigate, the chance for insight, a greater range of freedom and personal choice and, indeed, by implication, the moral responsibility which such an unfettering demands. However tenuously woven and fragile it may be, his fictions are increasingly imbued with a strand of hope. Concomitantly, there now exists—in all its psychological, moral, and religious ramifications—the possibility of personal salvation, an idea that in his darkest, most occluded years must have seemed to Carver fantastic.

Clearly, Raymond Carver's fiction is in flux. The stories in *Fires* and *Cathedral* seem to me richer, more emotionally and artistically complex than the earlier works. Permeated now by subtle shades of choice and option, Carver's "landscape of characters," as Robert Houston has fittingly called it in *The Nation*, resonates with an authenticity, a sense of the "real America," that was unrealized heretofore.[1] How great this philosophic and creative transformation is can be readily appreciated by a comparative detailing of the structures and "obsessions" (as Carver dislikes the term "themes") in stories like "The Bath" and its new version "A Small, Good Thing" and in the two variations of "So Much Water So Close to Home." In light of Carver's new, more optimistic version, these are fictions that, as he explained to Larry Mc-Caffery and Sinda Gregory (*Alive and Writing*, University of Illinois Press, 1987), were in clear need of being "enhanced, redrawn, reimagined" (69).

Like so many of the tales in *What We Talk About When We Talk About Love* and the other collections, "The Bath" focuses on the dilemmas engendered when, as Thomas R. Edwards has written in the *New York Review of Books*, "marginal lives are intruded upon by mystery, a sense of something larger or more elemental" than what has been previously experienced.[2] In "The Bath," with a stroke that is typically Carverian, this "mystery" is death—or, at least, the real possibility of it when a young boy, on his birthday, is struck by a hit-and-run car. Lapsing into a "sleep-like" state, the child lingers in the hospital, his terrified and confused parents hovering near. Their vigil, which would be horrifying enough, is further menaced when, on brief trips home to bathe and feed the dog, they are subjected to ominous calls "about Scotty" from a baker enraged about "the Birthday Boy's" expensive and now-forgotten cake.

Despite evidence of a genuinely loving domesticity and a somewhat affluent (at least, solidly middle-class) lifestyle, the characters in "The Bath" are nonetheless typical of Carver's "down-and-outers," his people on the verge. Like the rock-throwing protagonist in "Viewfinder" or the battling young parents in "Popular Mechanics," these folks are totems, faceless, nearly nameless emblems of a class. While the baker is deftly particularized by his "watery eyes" and the "curious apron," which loops about him in the fashion of a straight-jacket to end in a "very thick knot," the parents and child go without description. Two thirds of the way through the story, and then almost grudgingly, we are finally given a name for the family—Weiss. And while the mother's Christian name does manage to slip out in conversation, we are never told the father's.

Skeletally-drawn, the Weisses reveal little of themselves. Though they no doubt entertain vague, unspoken dreams—symbolically evidenced by the futuristic cake for Scotty with its rocketship and stars—they, and all the other characters here, are clearly enmeshed in the unexamined life. This is Carver's "real America": a netherland of work-place, home, and shopping centers. With junk food for the body (characteristically, Scotty is munching potato chips as he is struck) and even junkier sentiments for the soul (Scotty's young companion, holding the bag after his friend has crumpled in the gutter, actually wonders "if he should finish the rest or continue on to school"), perhaps it is easier not to think, not to question, to take the bad curves and good in life for granted. In "The Bath," it is the unnamed father who senses this. Driving home from the hospital "faster than he should," he dimly realizes that "It had been a good life till now. There had been work, fatherhood, family. He had been lucky and happy." But beyond this vaguely articulable grocery-list of good things, he seems unable to go. In the shadow of this overwhelming mystery, "Fear made him want to take a bath." And with this act, he tries, unsuccessfully, to wash all thought from him as though it were sin.

In "The Bath," this moment is the closest we come to insight, epiphany. But, true to the harsh parameters Carver has already drawn, it is brushed aside by the ritual cleansing and, of even greater import, the increasing menace from the outside world: that ringing phone, the unrecognized voice with its torturing accusations.

In a world where ordinary kindness seems so often proscribed, where the larger community seems simply not to exist, we are not surprised that understanding of the self and others is limited, communication negligible or, worse, mere "human noise" ("What We Talk About When We Talk About Love"). As the tale progresses towards its final horror, we witness growing confusion, an increasing inability to define and name. When the father suggests that the dog might need to be fed, the mother makes a counterproposal of calling the neighbors: "Someone will feed him if you ask them to." Trying to conjure a name, she cannot come up with one. Even the doctors shilly-shally with words, refusing to define the boy's condition, to say if it is "coma" or not. The parents admit to prayer about their son, but it seems clear that no one is listening. In the end, they are left in limbo: their child hovering in some unnameable state, caught between existence and extinction, while the phone rings a final time. "It's about Scotty," the voice tells them. "Yes, it's about Scotty."

Winner of the Carlos Fuentes Award for Fiction, "The Bath" is obviously a masterwork of American minimalism and a product of Carver's own early aesthetic: "Get in, get out. Don't linger. Go On."[3] Typical of the other stories in *What We Talk About*, the style admits "nothing vague, or blurred, no smoked-glass prose" (*Fires*, 28). Indeed, its language is so attenuated, so pared of ornament and intentional ambiguity, so stunningly bare, it is almost, as David Boxer and Cassandra Phillips have claimed, "photorealistic."[4] But however successful "The Bath" may be on its own minimalist terms—however mimetic, as Michael Gorra observes, its "intentional poverty [and] anorexia" of style is of "the spiritual poverty of [the] characters' lives"[5]—this story clearly represents for Carver an avenue now exhausted.

Halfway through the writing of *Cathedral*, in the bloom of his "second life,"[6] Carver revised the tale, a process which finally took him "into the heart of what the story is *about*" (*Fires*, 218). Three times the length of its parent-story, "A Small, Good Thing" concerns many of the same "obsessions" as "The Bath," but told by a richer, more generous voice, these "obsessions" are transfigured, mediated and tempered by genuine compassion.

In "A Small, Good Thing," Carver's "submerged population" begins to surface, moving out from the preoccupations of self to become aware of and even feel kinship to the larger community. Instead of ignoring the surly baker as she did in "The Bath," her attention then focused squarely upon the material object of the cake, this "reimagined" mother now searches for some common denominator. She studies his "coarse features." She wonders "if he's ever done anything else with his life besides being a baker." Trying to diminish the "uncomfortable" feeling his presence causes her, she examines her own life, as well as her own perception of his, looking for a mutual base: "She was a mother and thirty-three years old, and it seemed to her that everyone, especially someone the baker's age—a man old enough to be her father—must have children who'd gone through this special time of cakes and birthday parties. There must be that between them, she thought."[7] Equally revealing are the changes in the scene that immediately follows this encounter. When Scotty is struck, his friend now drops the potato chips and begins "to cry." Even the driver of the car evidences a certain moral awareness, stopping now "in the middle of the road," waiting, before he drives off, "until the boy got unsteadily to his feet . . . dazed, but [apparently] okay" (*Where*, 281).

As one would expect, the introduction into Carver's world of compassion, however shaky or seedling, proves to be a mixed blessing. While this new-found empathy considerably deepens the emotional scope of the characters, it also brings into their now less-marginal lives a greater share of pain. This becomes achingly clear in Carver's revision of the mother's encounter with the black family. Their loved one, Nelson, in surgery—victim of a senseless knifing—they, like the Weisses, are awaiting news. Accidentally stumbling upon them in a littered waiting room, the mother apologizes, then asks for directions to the elevator. This given, she suddenly blurts out the painful details of her story. In "The Bath," with a brush-stroke that is typical of the early Carver, the response to her agony is an impotent shake of the father's head, the self-enclosed utterance, "Our Nelson." In this one, almost perfunctorily-sketched scene, Carver, while acknowledging the universality of tragedy, dismisses the possibility of connection between the aggrieved, a sentiment which is reversed in "A Small, Good Thing." Here, in a scene that is greatly expanded, the characters engage in a mutually-felt sympathy, their discourse characterized by the give-and-take of genuine conversation. The grief briefly shared reverberates as the mother, returning to the hospital later, recreates the young girl she encountered in that room, silently warning her not to have children: "For God's sake, don't" (*Where*, 293).

If empathy pains, it also transfigures, creating in Carver's new world a contemporary *via dolorosa* by which the characters may trudge toward salvation. Once the imagination succeeds, as the mother's has, in breaking through the crust of self toward an honest realization of others, a host of options and possibilities suddenly arise. In Carver's recent work, this process of personal redemption begins—much like the Christian theology which seems increasingly, if eclectically, to inform it—with the word.

Their despairing, blue-collar mediocrity aside, if Carver's early protagonists have anything in common, it is, as Robert Houston has remarked, their "stunning inarticulateness." From the teenaged girl in "Why Don't You Dance?"—who, faced with the mystery of domestic dissolution, tries to "get it talked out" and eventually "quit[s] trying"—to the alcoholic L.D. in "One More Thing"—who, upon leaving his wife and daughter, wants to spit out *the* parting shot, but cannot for the life of him think "what it could possibly be"—the characters in *What We Talk About* display a remarkable, if sometimes gratuitous, aphasia. In "The Bath" this is exemplified by the baker's elliptical calls, by the physicians' inability to name the boy's condition, by perhaps even the narrator himself who, so masterfully effaced in Carver's stories, often flounders with the simplest words, describing, for example, a gurney (properly named in "A Small, Good Thing") as "a thing like a bed . . . a thing with wheels."[8]

In the new version, this poverty of language diminishes. With the artful exception of the baker, every major character is now named, an act which signals a critical turn in Carver's work, for by creating a world in which things *can* be named—explored and objectified by the communal activity of language—Carver allows and, in fact, demands of his characters a truer engagement. In "A Small, Good Thing," Dr. Francis can no longer hedge about Scotty's unnatural sleep; he must confront it and call it by its name: "coma." By the same token, the irrational guilt of the parents (beautifully symbolized in "The Bath," but unacknowledged by the protagonists) must also be tackled, with Ann now admitting to herself that "she felt she was in some obscure way responsible for what had happened to the child" (*Where*, 293). Indeed, even the "mystery" itself can be broached; eyed squarely and investigated with words, as Carver now, courageously, releases Scotty from his hellish half-existence.

Carver's rendering of the child's death and its ramifications points in a way few other scenes can, to the depth of change in his aesthetic and philosophic perspective. In the earlier stories, death is generally portrayed as a malign and ultimately unknowable force; like a bolt from the natural world, it blasts in at the finale to shatter the artificial parameters constructed around unexamined lives. Faced with this powerful, ill-defined specter, Carver's characters could manage little beyond a mute, uncomprehending horror. Certainly, this is Carl's befuddled reaction to the cat and its dead mouse in "What's in Alaska?"; it is Bill Jamison's response to the gratuitous violence in "Tell the Women We're Going"; arguably, it forms the underpinning of Bill Parker's last act in "After the Denim," when, faced with his wife's probable cancer, he sets to his embroidery, "stitch after stitch—making believe he was waving like the man on the keel." In this existential world of lives that are demonstrably "dust" (if we believe the salesman's slick spiel in "Collectors"), death was invariably the ultimate, scene-stealing rogue. It could not be fought, understood, or even questioned, and thus its presence marked the end of the story.

With "A Small, Good Thing," this paradigm of helpless resignation is abandoned as Carver not only confronts death here—a victory in itself—but goes on to record the life after, the agony and resulting growth of those who survive. Given Carver's "obsession" for equating the masked and inarticulate life with spiritual death, one would be hard pressed to conjure a more symbolically fitting demise than Scotty's, as the child rouses briefly from his coma, emits a harrowing and incomprehensible howl, then dies, victim of "a hidden occlusion" of the brain. That this death is, as the bewildered doctors report, "a one in a million circumstance" only serves to intensify the parents' horror (and our own), for by this detail Carver reiterates his belief that, even in this more optimistic universe, a blind and inexplicable randomness still lurks, shaping and destroying at will.

If, in human affairs, contingency plays a major role, it is no longer necessarily a decisive one. There are choices of response, Carver now makes clear, options, even the opportunity to fight back. And this is what Scotty's parents do. After a brief and expected period of stunned denial, the Weisses return home. Rejecting the impulse to box Scotty's toys, thus prolonging his denial of the child's death, Howard finds himself drawn to Ann. Sitting on the couch, he weeps; they embrace; she struggles to find the words that, in elucidating their new and horrible reality, will console. Finally, she tells him, "He's gone . . . Howard, he's gone. He's gone and now we'll have to get used to that. To being alone" (*Where*, 296). Later, phoning relatives, she seems to find some relief in the act of articulation, only to have this shattered when the phone rings, its disembodied voice demanding to know, "Have you forgotten Scotty?" (*Where*, 297).

Just before midnight, the torture resumes with yet another call to the Weisses; but this time, by virtue of her engagement with the old man in the story's opening scene, Ann is able to identify the menacing source without. "I know who it is!" she exclaims to Howard. "It's the baker, the son-of-a-bitching baker!" (*Where*, 298). With this knowledge, the stage is set for the final encounter.

In the middle of the night, the fake-icing stars of Scotty's cake now aptly transfigured into the real thing, the Weisses drive to the shopping center. In a tense scene, reminiscent of the repressed violence ubiquitous in Carver's early tales, the angry parents confront the baker, who in turn arms himself with his rolling pin. Feeling "a deep burning inside her, an anger that made her feel larger than herself, larger than either of these men" (*Where*, 299), the mother spits out the reason for the abandoned cake, the story of Scotty's death. By articulating her pain, she is released from her murderous rage; amid tears and a growing nausea, she cries out for response, saying, "It isn't fair!" (*Where*, 300).

While God or the Fates may be unmoved by the Weisses' private disaster, the baker clearly is not. In the stark radiance of another's grief, his own "hidden occlusion"—a mask erected by years of loneliness and failure—is brought to light, begins dissolving as he discards the pin, unties the heavy apron. Drawn into this mode of confession, he apologizes for his boorish behavior, even seeks to understand it as, in a monologue reminiscent of the mother's frantic speech to the black family, he unburdens himself, recounting to the Weisses the pain of his solitary life. Finally, he invites the couple to sit down and eat, for "Eating is a small good thing in a time like this" (*Where*, 301).

If Carver's titles are intended to suggest the essence of his fictions, it is apparent that the major "obsessions" of "A Small, Good Thing" are vastly different from those of "The Bath." While the earlier story, with its Old Testament image of *mikvah*, or ritual cleansing, hinges upon the despair of a guilt which cannot be washed away, a grief that stands no chance of utterance and resolution, the revised version, like Scripture itself, strives for something better, a new covenant between the players: the chance for salvation through communion. Surely, this is the "message" of the final scene with the baker offering the suffering couple "cinnamon rolls just out of the oven," coffee, conversation, then a dark, heavy bread which he "break[s] open" like the Eucharist. As the boundaries between them are chipped away through this sharing of bread and pain, the characters find, even in a world that seems fundamentally artificial, transcendence of a sort, for "It was like daylight under the fluorescent trays of light. They talked on into the early morning, the high, pale cast of light in the windows, and they did not think of leaving" (*Where*, 301).

The hopeful sensibility now permeating much of Carver's newest fiction is not without its critics. To be sure, Carver has been accused of falling prey, in his post-alcoholic years, to "sentimentality"; but this assessment, I think, misses the point. In *Cathedral* and *Fires*, there are still no easy answers. Beyond the tingling vagaries of human thought and speech, there is no clear road to salvation for anyone. Indeed, now more than ever, victory seems a relative thing, dependent as much upon the point of departure as upon the destination.

This becomes clear when we look at the two versions of "So Much Water So Close to Home." In the original tale, published in *What We Talk About*, Carver's protagonist, Claire, must face a horrible truth: that for an entire weekend her husband, Stuart, and his friends—"decent men, family men, men who take care of their jobs" (*What*, 80–81)—ignored the body of a young rape victim floating in the Naches River where they had come to fish. While their behavior is callous, verging at times upon the incredible, it is nevertheless typical of Carver's incapacitants who, by denying death, refuse confrontation with the greater "mystery." Obviously, Claire is appalled by her husband's insensitivity. Shaken by his inability to distinguish between right and wrong, she begins to identify with the murdered girl, even going so far as to attend the funeral. Yet, beyond a temporary rebuffing of her boorish mate, she can manage little else by way of a personal response. Finally, by story's close, she spins her own web of denial, seeking to obliterate the entire moral dilemma with a loveless and hurried act of sex.

The new version in *Fires*, twice as long as the original, presents a greatly enhanced, more complex situation. Generous with specific detail, Carver now shows us more of the lost weekend, how, in a scenario symbolically dovetailing the events following the Passion, these good soldiers attempt to erase from their consciences the reality of—and, by default, their complicity in—the girl's death. From Friday to Sunday, these "decent men" drink; they gamble with cards; they tell each other "coarse stories." They continue to fish, cooking and eating their catch, even washing their plates scant feet from the body. But as strong as their denial of the "mystery" is, they cannot maintain the illusion of ignorance forever. On Saturday night, we are told that "no one mentioned the girl until Gordon Johnson, who'd forgotten for a minute, commented on the firmness of the trout they'd caught, and the terrible coldness of the river water" (*Where*, 162). Falling silent then, they continue to drink "until one of them tripped and fell cursing against the lantern . . ." (*Where*, 162). The next afternoon, "a day earlier than they'd planned," they decide to leave; driving in silence, they finally reach a public phone where Stuart spills out the grisly details of their discovery to the police.

When she learns, later, of her husband's grim adventure, Claire is confounded. Like the "reimagined" mother of "A Small, Good Thing," she now possesses a greater emotional and imaginative capacity, enabling her to resurrect the entire scene from Stuart's grudging details. But this creative ability, this engagement with the truth of things, brings with it greater risk. And as she tries to ferret through the mess—wondering, for instance, if it were Stuart who, in an attempt to keep the body from floating away, tied the girl's hand to a tree—she finds herself on dangerous ground, a *terra incognita* which she, already the victim of one nervous breakdown, may not be able to negotiate.

As the story progresses, Claire's quest for the truth begins to take on the form of a high-wire act: trying to stay aloft, she treads a very thin line, attempting to balance the growing and ever more disturbing set of interior realizations against the demands of her family and the community at large. Certain that "1) people no longer care what happens to other people; and 2) nothing makes any real difference any longer" (*Where*, 167)—the very prescription of Carver's early, minimalist world!—Claire nevertheless tramps on, disproving in the process her own despairing theory. She confronts her husband repeatedly, demanding (once actually trying to slap it out of him) answers that he is unwilling or unable to give. Though she realizes that "This is crazy. . . . We need to lock our fingers together. We need to help one another" (*Where*, 166), she distances herself from him, moving first to the sofa, then to her child's room, finally to the spare bedroom to sleep.

In the midst of this, and ever-mindful of Stuart's part warning that one day "this affair" of their marriage "will end in violence" (*Where*, 168), Claire becomes aware of the profound connections within the larger community. The dead girl is identified now; she has a name ("Susan Miller"), a face (sweetly smiling in a high school portrait), a family (whose grief is ghoulishly captured for broadcast on the nightly news). Her death diminishes everyone. It heightens fear and suspicion, feelings acutely experienced by Claire who becomes "afraid, so afraid" and now worries that something might happen to her son. Still worse, Claire senses her own precarious position, for while the dead are irreplaceable, the living, clearly, are not; and Claire knows that should her odyssey become too unmanageable, too bizarre, her judgmental mother-in-law stands ready to take her place, this time perhaps permanently.

Given this climate, Claire's efforts (including her hundred-mile trek on a dangerous road to the funeral) begin to take on the sheen of the heroic. But if this is heroism, it is not in the least sentimentally conceived or executed. Informed as she is by the belief that "nothing will change for Stuart and me . . . nothing will ever really be any different" (*Where*, 167), Claire does not find the answers she seeks. Indeed, she almost succumbs once more to the tempting hammock of denial when, in the final scene, Stuart threatens her, saying on the phone that he's asked "mother to come stay with us for a few days." Claire hangs up, but dials his number a moment later, saying, "It doesn't matter, Stuart. Really, I tell you it doesn't matter one way or the other." His protestation of "love" briefly lulls her; she feels, as so many of Carver's characters have when faced with similar crises, "sleepy." But awareness that has been striven for and earned cannot be so easily dismissed. Carver knows this, as we do, just as Claire herself dimly perceives as she suddenly "wake[s] up," saying, "For God's sake, Stuart, she was only a child" (*Where*, 177).

If this final act comprises a victory for Claire, it is arguably a small one, possibly even Pyrrhic. Her statement seems automatic; its effect on Stuart and their marriage is uncertain. In truth, it resolves nothing beyond the expression of her desire to confront the "mystery," to articulate her feelings and ideas about this frightening, fantastic, intrusive thing with whatever words she can find.

And maybe this is enough. Like the characters in "A Small, Good Thing"—indeed, like so many of the folk populating Carver's new landscape—perhaps Claire finds release in the telling, if not salvation then at least a clear sign about which direction to now pursue. In this, she exemplifies the true "heart" of what Carver's recent stories are "about." And while we may be sure, as Raymond Carver appears to be, that the act of articulation is not, in and of itself, a panacea for the grief and staggering uncertainty to which we are heir, we are reminded in these tales that the word, honestly uttered, constitutes a beginning, some place from which to start.

Notes

1. Robert Houston, "A Stunning Inarticulateness," *Nation*, 4 July 1981, 23.
2. Thomas R. Edwards, "The Short View: *Will You Please Be Quiet, Please?*" *New York Review of Books*, 1 April 1976, 35.
3. *Fires: Essays, Poems, Stories* (New York: Vintage Books, 1984): 13; hereafter cited in the text as *Fires*.
4. David Boxer and Cassandra Phillips, "*Will You Please Be Quiet, Please?*: Voyeurism, Dissociation, and the Art of Raymond Carver," *Iowa Review* 10, no. 3 (Summer 1979): 81.
5. Michael Gorra, "Laughter and Bloodshed," *Hudson Review* 37 (Spring 1984): 155.
6. Larry McCaffery and Sinda Gregory, eds. *Alive and Writing: Interviews with American Authors of the 1980s* (Urbana, Ill.: University of Illinois Press, 1987), 68; hereafter cited in the text as *Alive*.
7. Raymond Carver, *Where I'm Calling From: New and Selected Stories* (New York: Atlantic Monthly Press, 1988), 280; hereafter cited in the text as *Where*.
8. ———, *What We Talk about When We Talk about Love* (New York: Alfred A. Knopf, 1981), 53; hereafter cited in the text as *What*.

Mark A. R. Facknitz

In a recent symposium on contemporary American fiction, Raymond Carver wondered "who isn't tired to death by now of that stale debate" over minimalism.[1] Indeed, though no minimalist writer is willing to accept the label, paradoxically an unspecifiable minimalism has become one of the reigning commonplaces of our day, and—like "dirty realism" and photo-realism, with which it shares many characteristics— it is now so thoroughly ordinary that television programs like *Miami Vice* and *Moonlighting* freely partake of reductive and allusive techniques that minimalist fiction writers are generally assumed to have been the first to use. Quick cuts, elliptical dialogue, blunt ironies, and plain surfaces as narrative devices originate in a tradition of short story writing that goes back through Hemingway to Chekhov and Maupassant, and few will be offended by the assertion that minimalism in fiction is a reflection of the fragmentary and alienated condition of the twentieth-century self. This is the old news of modernism. But I suggest that ultimately the problem we lament lies not in minimalist craft but

From "Raymond Carver and the Menace of Minimalism," *CEA Critic* 52, nos. 1–2 (Fall 1989–Winter 1990): 62–73. © 1990 *CEA Critic*. Reprinted by permission. The documentation has been altered to conform with that of this book.

in a vision of the world that minimalist technique is wholly adequate to describe. Minimalism, more than any other technique, emphasizes to the point of cruelty the shortfall between the gifts of the world and our desire for plenitude.

In *The Lonely Voice*, Frank O'Connor confesses that he is frequently exasperated by Hemingway's limited scope. To O'Connor, the "clean, well-lighted place" may be merely empty—timeless, unpopulated, immune to the humanity of the voices that drift across the page. "In a charitable mood," O'Connor writes, "I sometimes find myself thinking of the clean well-lighted place as the sort of stage on which Racine's heroes and heroines appear, free of contact with common things, and carrying on their lofty discussions of what to Racine seemed most important."[2] But while the sparse unities and clear lines of classicism may inspire occasional concessions, O'Connor's attitude is volatile, and he is apt to decide that "this wonderful technique of Hemingway's is really a technique in search of a subject, and searching all the time for a clean well-lighted place where all the difficulties of human life can be comfortably ignored" (O'Connor, 169). In short, O'Connor suspects Hemingway of being nihilistic as well as artless. In his guise as Racine, Hemingway succeeds at depicting his characters as rootless and disembodied members of a caste deprived of tradition and family. Or, perhaps, Hemingway may merely be funking his responsibility to understand a real human situation, one in which his characters ought to be endowed with free will, a past, and a sense of purpose.

Yet, for Hemingway technique was a form of purgation of dishonesty, a means of ridding the story of extraneous background that might inhibit rather than promote the search for truth. In *A Moveable Feast*, he recalls his apprenticeship days in Paris when he would tell himself: " 'Do not worry. You have always written before and you will write now. All you have to do is write one true sentence. Write the truest sentence you know.' So finally I would write one true sentence, and then go on from there. It was easy because there was always one true sentence that I knew or had seen or had heard someone say."[3]

Whatever was cut or rejected before it went on paper Hemingway characterized as "scrollwork or ornament," disfiguring embellishment, and to the extent that his short stories are the principal models of minimalist fiction, minimalists must be seen as writers who draw the boundaries of truth and concern themselves only with the matter that lies within.

In O'Connor's ambivalence, we discover a frustration he has in common with many readers of current minimalist fiction. For if art cannot satisfy our desire to be raised out of quotidian existence, then art apparently doesn't amount to much. Above all, complain such readers, minimalist art does not require moral involvement—not the author's, not the reader's. The key precept of minimalism appears to be precisely this requirement that the work be stripped of judgment and invite no judgment; the minimalist work deletes any sign of the work's having an intention upon us. The short story, then, is the preeminent minimalist literary form, for if there is scarcely time to develop a round character in a short story, there is even less time to moralize. By the tightness of its focus, the short story inevitably alienates characters from their larger lives, or, as Frank O'Connor puts it, the story renders them "symbolically divorced from their normal surroundings and friends" (O'Connor, 24). The Hemingway stories—especially, perhaps, the touchstone texts of "A Clean, Well-Lighted Place," "Hills Like White Elephants," and "Cat in the Rain"—exaggerate the short story's natural hostility to fullness, most obviously in their ostentatious elimination of moral judgments.

In the works of Raymond Carver, this tendency creates a peculiar tension. If he is a minimalist, Carver is so in part because he scrupulously removes himself from any posture that might imply the presence of a moralizing author. His characters, however, are universally the victims of the death of morality; they are haunted by the absence of spiritual value and live restless and terrified in a moral void. Readers of Carver are apt to find his stories either fascinating or irritating. In reviewing Carver's second collection of stories, *What We Talk About When We Talk About Love* (1981), James Atlas of *The Atlantic* complained that Carver's "characters are hardly garrulous; their talk is groping, rudimentary,"[4] and essentially they have nothing to say to one another. Less *is* less, Atlas says, and "minimality" may offer the stories "bleak power' only if the reader generously fills in the gaps caused by the author's absence and the character's lack of eloquence. Finally, such "perfect economy" insists that "the writer's responsibility is only to register what is true in a literal, documentary sense" (Atlas, 97).

Several readers have tried to see the contemporary trend of minimalism as a phenomenon of the marketplace. Robert Dunn in *The New York Times Book Review* writes of it as "fiction that shrinks from life," or what he calls "private interest fiction," the fiction of the Reagan era, simplistic and self-satisfied, which "turns inward and finds a paucity, a confusion, an absence," and which "fails to engage the expansive possibilities of our lives."[5] Dan Pope, writing in *The Gettysburg Review*, sees

Carver's popularity as "an influence that has swamped literary journals with blue collar heroes, mobile homes, Kentucky Fried chicken dinners, and characters named Bob or Bill or Bud."[6] Madison Bell makes a similar argument. In a 1986 essay for *Harper's*, he revives James Atlas's title "Less Is Less," which Atlas himself borrowed from Joshua Gilder of the *New Criterion*, and Bell proposes that in attempting to compete with film, fiction has found itself at the absurd limits of technical extremism. The minimalists, says Bell, are supremely commercial writers, driven not by artistic necessity but by advertising's need for easy blurbs and homogeneity, as well as the entertainment industry's tendency to define audiences by the lowest common denominator. Carver and a growing number of minimalist writers—Robison, Phillips, Hempel, Leavitt, and others—define for Bell "an excessively small literary world, one in which everyone tends to resemble everyone else," and whose members cultivate "an obsessive concern for surface detail, a tendency to ignore or eliminate distinctions among people it renders, and a studiedly deterministic, at times nihilistic, vision of the world."[7] A practitioner such as Ann Beattie is blistered for making "nonsense of personal freedom and personal responsibility" while her characters are "people reduced to a single common attribute of casual despair" (Bell, 66). Raymond Carver's story "Bridle" gets rapped for "dime-store determinism" (Bell, 66), and finally, when less is less, much becomes nothing in the view of readers like Bell.

Particularly in Carver's case, it is difficult to demonstrate that despair is merely superficial, and many readers find Carver's minimalism telling beyond the measures of techniques. Even a generally hostile critic such as Joe David Bellamy will admit that below the surface there "lies a morass of inarticulated yearnings and unexamined horrors, repressed violence, the creeping certainty that nothing matters."[8] William Stull situates Carver's stories in "Hopelessville, USA, the contemporary counterpart of Sherwood Anderson's Winesburg, Ohio,"[9] and he concedes that "at its narrowest, . . . [Carver's] writing can be acerbic, mannered and predictable" (Stull, 3). Through Carver's second collection, *What We Talk About When We Talk About Love*, and for most of the stories in *Cathedral* (1983), Stull's judgment applies: Raymond Carver is an author whose characters fail to communicate and so reveal "a heartfelt pessimism, a conviction that things never are and never can be what they should be" (Stull, 3). But Stull continues. The stories nevertheless can have an "unsettling immediacy" and "haunting verisimilitude" (Stull, 3), characteristics that Ewing Campbell, in "Raymond Carver and the Literature of Subtraction," defines as Carver's ability to endow the "spoken word with subsurface values" and "to create deceptive originality behind the facade of the commonplace."[10] In defending Carver, Campbell decides that the "literature of subtraction" does not degenerate into a fiction of mere surface and silliness but instead becomes "the literature of multiple levels, multiple meanings, and even multiple threats" (Campbell, 71). Minimalist technique, then, may be a sure sign of submerged menace.

Carver's evaluation is simple. He writes, "I think a little menace is fine to have in a story"; it is "good for the circulation."[11] In the same essay, "On Writing," he explains that he derives most of his effects from the failure of memory and the serendipities of composition. He feels his way into a story, making himself susceptible to intuition and chance. Once, when his writing was interrupted with a phone call, a sinister voice asking for someone named Nelson, Carver found his story invaded by a vague and threatening character of the same name. Thus, Carver moves from line to line like a man groping in the dark, depending heavily on chance to help him find his way. Carver elaborates: "I make up the conversations in my stories. I put the furnishings and the physical things surrounding people into the stories as I need those things. Perhaps this is why it's sometimes been said that my stories are unadorned, stripped down, even 'minimalist.' But maybe it's nothing more than a working marriage of necessity and convenience that has brought me to writing the kind of stories I do in the way I do" (*Fires*, 21).

In a practical sense, therefore, Carver's stories do appear to emerge more from an attitude than from a method, or at least the method appears to be a way of holding oneself open to the suggestions of coincidence and the subconscious mind, and of limiting oneself to such suggestions and little else. Marilynne Robinson makes a similar point in her review of Carver's most recent collection. Writing on *Where I'm Calling From: New and Selected Stories* (1988), she argues:

> Mr. Carver uses his narrow world to generate suggestive configurations that could not occur in a wider one. His impulse to simplify is like an attempt to create a hush, not to hear less, but to hear better. Nothing recurs so powerfully in these stories as the imagination of another life, always so like the narrator's or the protagonist's own that the imagination of it is an experience of the self, that fuddled wraith. It is as if the replication of the conditions of one's life in

another's rescued one from the terrors of accident and randomness, as if the germ of myth and archetype were found at work in the tepid plasma of unstructured experience.[12]

But this takes Carver at his best, and in all of his collections there are stories that only devoted and generous readers could characterize as having mythic or archetypal traces of anything. More typically, Carver's minimalism appears to deconstruct self-consciously the idea of an anagogic dimension as characters watch insects in moonlight or drink several bottles of champagne each day to wean themselves from hard liquor. On the other hand, even in the early collections there are a few stories in which characters at least dimly guess at lives fuller than their own.

Though Carver built his early reputation on strikingly small and pessimistic stories, many readers responded with relief as soon as a few stories showed a contrary impulse. Almost all academic commentary on Carver focuses on two stories from *Cathedral,* the title story and "A Small, Good Thing." William Stull's "Beyond Hopelessville" looks at "A Small, Good Thing," a revision of the old stripped-down story "The Bath," and concludes, in a paraphrase of Thomas Hardy's "Hap" (1898), that "what Carver first published as an existentialist tale of crass casualty he . . . offers anew as a story of spiritual rebirth, a minor masterpiece of humanist realism" (Stull, 13). I make similar points about "The Train," "A Small, Good Thing," and "Cathedral" in my essays in *Studies in Short Fiction;*[13] and in a recent essay, "Narrative Displacement and Literary Faith: Raymond Carver's Inheritance from Flannery O'Connor," Barbara Lonnquist decides that "perhaps [Carver's] final inheritance from Flannery O'Connor has been her invincible faith, after all,"[14] suggesting that his most powerful and widely anthologized stories assert that no situation is ever really hopeless.

In "Finding the Words: The Struggle for Salvation in the Fiction of Raymond Carver," Kathleen Westfall Shute assesses Carver's early career with the comment that his characters "were bankrupted, pink-slipped, often left to stumble alone through a detritus that was at core artificial and peculiarly American."[15] They were, she writes, "enmeshed in the unexamined life" and generally victims of an America that is "a netherland of workplace, home, and shopping centers" (Shute, 3). In analyzing two major revisions, however—"The Bath," which becomes "A Small, Good Thing," and the original and expanded versions of "So Much Water So Close to Home"—Shute emphasizes that the revisions reveal a stymied impulse to seek the redemptive moment or recognition that, in her words, finally "resolves nothing beyond the expression of [a] desire to confront the 'mystery'" (Shute, 9). But small victories amount to large gestures in Carver's work, and, particularly for readers who followed his course from story to story through the seventies and eighties, the emergence of a theme of salvation meant a considerable readjustment, for what had been a landscape of spiritual emptiness now held the minimal but very real promise of spiritual discovery.

The earliest of such interpretations were abetted by rumors that at long last Carver had come to grips with alcoholism. To put a cap on such hypotheses, in the *Paris Review* interview Carver stated that "Cathedral" was "totally different in conception and execution" from his previous work. He went on to comment: "When I wrote 'Cathedral' I experienced this rush and I felt, 'This is what it's all about, this is the reason we do this.' It was different than the stories that had come before. There was an opening up when I wrote the story. I knew I'd gone as far the other way as I could or wanted to go, cutting down to the bone. Any farther in that direction and I'd be at a dead end—writing stuff and publishing stuff I wouldn't want to read myself, and that's the truth" (*Fires*, 204).

In other words, what had been a technical manner and a means of discovering the essences of stories had become a personal dead end, a *reductio ad absurdum* of craft and heart. Clearly, in "Cathedral" and "A Small, Good Thing" Carver turns away from the cramped determinism of previous works. Yet, there was no golden age. Once Carver's language and vision offered his characters a new breadth of being, there arose a new threat, the great risk that they would be incapable of making anything of their freedom. Where once characters could resign themselves to the silly despondencies of complete loss, in the new mode they had to wonder anxiously when their chance to be lifted out of misery and meaninglessness would come.

In the fall of 1987, Carver had two-thirds of his left lung removed, then underwent radiation treatments for cancer that made work difficult in the last year of his life.[16] Six months before, he had delivered the manuscript of his most recent collection to his editor.[17] Without knowing it, Carver was selecting for posterity his favorite stories as well as seven previously uncollected stories. In *Where I'm Calling From: New and Selected Stories*, two of the new works, "Intimacy" and "Whoever Was Using This Bed," show Carver seeming to regress to a pre-*Cathe-*

dral manner, indulging himself in the kind of torpid kookiness that characterized *Will You Please Be Quiet, Please?* and *What We Talk About When We Talk About Love.* Indeed, the stories read like self-parodies. But in other of the new stories, Carver is taking risks and seeking a plenitude comparable to that he achieves in "A Small, Good Thing" and "Cathedral." For example, the narrator of "Boxes" finds the sudden equanimity required to address his neurotic and deeply unhappy mother as "Dear." The protagonist of "Elephant," another epiphanic story, experiences an ambivalent but powerful rush of freedom from guilt and responsibility. However, set beside the earlier redemptive stories, these provide markedly less closure and more ambiguity. If anything, they are intent on placing insight in a wholly ironic and inferior mode, rejecting the optimism of the previous epiphanic stories in favor of a more cynical view that a fortunate few fools are occasionally possessed by sudden bliss.

Two other stories, "Blackbird Pie" and "Errand," a biographical fantasy on the death of Anton Chekhov, seem to mark a new and more sophisticated tendency in Carver's work, in particular a willingness to seek his characters outside the lower classes in late twentieth-century America. In "Blackbird Pie," Carver uses a distinctly antiminimalist voice, the only clear instance in his work when he distinguishes between narrator and implied author. In "Blackbird Pie," Carver's protagonist struggles with the discrepancy between the "plain" facts of the past and the inescapable but incredible events of the present. In "Errand," Carver himself abolishes the lines between biography and fiction, shifting imperceptibly from history, through possibility, to speculation. In each of these stories, Carver achieves something new, and most important he does it in spite of the menace of an old fatuity that "Intimacy" and "Whoever Was Using This Bed" do not elude.

In "Menudo," Carver confronts the threat of senselessness head on. He works with old themes: adultery, alcoholism, insomnia, the febrility of memory, and the lurking menace of meaninglessness. In the story, a man wanders the house while his wife sleeps. He looks across the street to the house of Amanda, his lover, and he imagines her sitting in pink slippers in a leather chair with full ashtrays around her. He sees, in short, a few physical appurtenances but nothing of her, and he reflects with glib irony, "We're nice people, of all us, to a point."[18] As he waits for morning, the narrator recalls a past whose pernicious patterns seem to be reasserting themselves. Currently in his second marriage, he watches it break up in a way similar to the first. His first wife, whom he calls "this girl I started out with in life, this sweet thing, this gentle soul" (*Where*, 342), had become increasingly alienated as the marriage deteriorated and had thrown herself into an arcane quest for meaning. The narrator remembers that "she wound up going to fortune-tellers, palm readers, *crystal ball gazers*, looking for answers, trying to figure out what she should do with her life" (*Where*, 342–43). In fact, she became so controlled by her appetite for meaning that she quit her teaching job, wore weird clothing, and tried to levitate, as if the ability to rise physically implied the ability of the spirit to transcend uncertainty and hurt. No sooner does the narrator relate the first wife's search than he betrays the emptiness of his own spirit: "When Molly and I were growing up together, she was a part of me and sure, I was a part of her, too. We loved each other. It *was* our destiny. I believed in it myself. But now I don't know what to believe in. I'm not complaining, simply stating a fact. I'm down to nothing. And I have to go on like this. No destiny. Just the next thing meaning whatever you think it does. Compulsion and error, just like everyone else" (*Where*, 343).

The narrator of "Menudo" appears to be a perfect candidate for the kind of transforming insight granted to the narrator of "Cathedral" and to the Weisses of "A Small, Good Thing."

In fact, the open question that provides this plot with its forward motion is whether or not the poor soul will be handed understanding. As he drinks warm milk and watches the house across the street, the narrator does penance, poking away at some guilt left from a bit of stinginess that his mother's sudden death made it impossible for him to reconcile, and then he falls into a recollection of his drinking days: "One night I was at my friend Alfredo's house, a bunch of us drinking and listening to records. I didn't care any longer what happened to me. Everything, I thought, that could happen had happened. I felt unbalanced. I felt lost" (*Where*, 347).

He is overtaken by a bad case of the shakes, and to calm and nourish him Alfredo sets about making a pot of menudo. But as the stew simmers, the narrator is overpowered by the alcohol. He goes into a spare room, passes out, sleeps until midday, and wakes to find that all the menudo is eaten and everyone is gone. In "Cathedral," a revelation comes to a booze-blunted creature, giving him through human touch fundamental insight into the spaciousness of the human spirit, and in "A Small, Good Thing" Ann and Howard Weiss begin to have their terrible grief alleviated by the power of several obvious symbols of the

Eucharist, particularly the bread the once villainous baker serves them. But there is no such communion in "Menudo." The narrator and Alfredo drift apart, the gap between them as unbridgeable as those between the narrator and his mother, his first wife, and, now, his second wife.

"Menudo" is not about salvation but about a soul who waits for it, wants it, and needs it, but misses his few slim chances. Indeed, this narrator seems to be a holdover from Carver's early fiction, for though he has dried himself out, he continues to be the victim of fate and desire, driven toward one woman while still in love with another. For all his will-power, he is unable to conquer the dreadful anomie that he once escaped through drinking. Within the boundaries of the story, there is no hope for a bright new prospect. Instead, at dawn we find him acting like a postmodern Candide, raking his own yard and then, because he must do something while waiting, moving next door to rake the Baxter's yard. But Baxter, "a decent, ordinary guy," has no idea how to interpret the presence of his neighbor in his front yard early in the morning, though of course there may be lunacy and danger in it. As Baxter pulls off in his car, he raises his hand in what "could be a salute or a sign of dismissal" (*Where*, 350). In the manner of the blind man in "Cathedral," the gesture could be a blessing, but for the moment the narrator cannot tell. He has been on his knees pulling leaves into a bag, and he waves back, or rather makes a gesture that he calls "not a wave, exactly, but close to it." Someone he does not recognize drives by and "gives his horn a friendly little tap," and the story closes with the narrator crossing the street in the direction of his lover's house.

This world is potentially compassionate, but the main characters of "Menudo," "Blackbird Pie," "Boxes," and "Elephant" must live in doubt, offered and offering obscure signs, crossing streets without a clear sense of purpose and under the threat that they are simply making old mistakes over again. In their ambivalence, then, these stories appear to be a return to an old minimalist manner and message. But like Carver's redemptive stories, they take their time, they furnish themselves with neighbors, friends, lovers, food, night and dawn, mysticism and doubt—that is to say, the symbolic conditions necessary to a redemptive story—and they have heroes who need understanding and freedom as badly as anyone could. Finally, these new protagonists deserve saving, for they struggle—with varying degrees of awareness—to keep themselves open to the sudden invasion of feeling and meaning.

In "Menudo," the man cultivates his own garden and his neighbor's, hoping for the revelation that, in this best of all possible worlds, there is ultimately some peace for the lonely sufferer.

But does any of this mean that there really is such a thing as minimalism, either as a literary school of which Carver may be a founder though not, ultimately, a fellow, or as a set of techniques that some writers employ in greater and lesser measures, depending on the local demands of the story they are writing? So slippery is the question, and so firm is the assumption that there is such a thing, that in 1985 the *Mississippi Review* devoted a double issue to minimalism without really offering a satisfactory definition. John Barth, though able to offer a paradigm for minimalism in Bauhaus architecture and the sculpture of Gaudier-Brezska and Constantine Brancusi, was unable to find a theoretical center to a literary manner unlike his own but toward the practitioners of which he felt considerable sympathy. Potential literary minimalisms were so plentiful that the term was useless: "There are minimalisms of style: a stripped-down vocabulary; a stripped-down syntax that avoids periodic sentences, serial predications and complex subordinating constructions; a stripped-down rhetoric that may eschew figurative language altogether; a stripped-down, non-emotive tone. And there are minimalisms of material: minimal characters, minimal exposition ('all that David Copperfield kind of crap,' says J. D. Salinger's catcher in the rye), minimal *mises en scene*, minimal action, minimal plot."[19]

Frederick Barthelme, in "On Being Wrong: Convicted Minimalist Spills Bean," comes as close as anyone to accepting the heavy/light mantle of minimalism. The essay is funny and autobiographical, and so the assumption that the crucial moment for contemporary fiction came in a series of workshops in the MFA program at Johns Hopkins in the early seventies is not to be taken seriously. The general import of Barthelme's argument is a different matter, however. For Barthelme, most of the neorealists who are accused of minimalism came of age in the sixties, a slap-happy time when stapling a bag of dirt inside a text "recontextualized the prose,"[20] but while the major writers of the decade (Barth, Hawkes, Gass, and Pynchon, for example) could pull off self-reflexive fiction with flair, the efforts of their imitators led to a disillusionment with a literary art that seemed ever more zany and frail. Thus, the generation of writers who began to publish in the seventies sought a manner that was free of clowning and a realism free of the taint of big ideas, to them a lamentable quality of late nineteenth- and early twentieth-century fiction. Like Hemingway, Barthelme sees fiction as a way of putting readers into the lives of characters with the minimum possible mediation, and he comments that "mostly what's going on with this new fiction" is that writers and their preferred readers are "rolling down the windows, trying to get a good whiff of what's out there" (Barthelme, 27). The objective, finally, is as old as Sophocles and Aristophanes: to leave room for the spectator's imagination, and to break the heart or to make it sing.

There is a minimalism at least in the sense that readers, enthusiastic as well as deprecatory, think that there is. But minimality is teleological, not technical, and its threat is not a local hazard of contemporary letters but a general and menacing character of the age. In this sense, it appears in the works of Jayne Anne Phillips, in which young characters speak in a discourse of psychological platitudes, the most common form of closure a vague regret over the large losses that characters do not have the courage or desire to confront; in the works of Jay McInerney, in which glitz is all one gets and all one has the right to want; in the works of Richard Ford, in which violence and defeat often appear the *a priori* conditions of human life; and in the works of Bobbie Ann Mason, in whose stories the television is always on, and whose characters adopt the meager nostrums of Phil Donahue and the commonplace values of commercials as if they constituted all the spiritual integument one could need or want.

My argument is that in Carver's career the menace migrated from world view to the world itself, and the representative late stories function as tragic allegories in which large souls strive for freedom in a world of excessively narrow formal constraints. Where minimalism was before a literary manner, a technique whose possibilities drove meaning to the limit of terrifying silliness, minimalism defined as a narrowness or poverty of spirit has become the chief threat in Carver's work. Minimalism now represents the ultimate antagonist, a nihilistic monster that has the potential of overwhelming the protagonist with silence, stillness, and senselessness. No longer is minimalism Hemingway's manner of suggesting the world's mysterious extensity by what is left out; instead, Carver's recent fictions press forward as if driven by the fear of discovering that there is no mystery and that minimalist technique may be wholly sufficient to describe the truth of the human heart. Thus, the implied reader shares the position of Carver's nameless narrators, waiting to see the rescue but departing the story without knowing for certain what any of the signs have meant.

Notes

1. Nicholas Delbanco, ed., "A Symposium on Contemporary American Fiction," *Michigan Quarterly Review* 24, no. 4 (1987): 711.

2. Frank O'Connor, *The Lonely Voice: A Study in the Short Story* (New York: Harper-Colophon, 1985), 169; hereafter cited in the text as O'Connor.

3. Ernest Hemingway, *A Moveable Feast* (New York: Charles Scribner's Sons, 1964), 12.

4. James Atlas, "Less Is Less," *Atlantic Monthly*, June 1981, 97; hereafter cited in the text as Atlas.

5. Robert Dunn, "Fiction That Shrinks from Life," *New York Times Book Review*, 30 June 1985, 24.

6. Dan Pope, "The Post-Minimalist American Story or What Comes after Carver?" *The Gettysburg Review* 1, no. 2 (1988): 332.

7. Madison Bell, "Less Is Less," *Harper's*, April 1986, 65; hereafter cited in the text as Bell.

8. Joe David Bellamy, *"Will You Please Be Quiet, Please?" Harper's Bookletter*, 26 April 1976.

9. William Stull, "Beyond Hopelessville: Another Side of Raymond Carver," *Philological Quarterly* 64, no. 1 (Winter 1985): 2; hereafter cited in the text as Stull.

10. Ewing Campbell, "Raymond Carver and the Literature of Subtraction," *Balcones Review* 1, no. 1 (1987): 70; hereafter cited in the text as Campbell.

11. *Fires: Essays, Poems, Stories* (New York: Vintage Books, 1984), 17; hereafter cited in the text as *Fires*.

12. Marilynne Robinson, "Marriage and Other Astonishing Bonds," *New York Times Book Review*, 15 May 1988, 35.

13. See Mark Facknitz, "'The Calm,' 'A Small, Good Thing,' and 'Cathedral': Raymond Carver and the Recovery of Human Worth," *Studies in Short Fiction* 23, no. 3 (1986): 287–96; and Mark Facknitz, "Missing the Train: Raymond Carver's Sequel to John Cheever's 'The Five-Forty-Eight,'" *Studies in Short Fiction* 22, no. 3 (1985): 345–47.

14. Barbara Lonnquist, "Narrative Displacement and Literary Faith: Raymond Carver's Inheritance from Flannery O'Connor," in *Since Flannery O'Connor: Essays on the Contemporary American Short Story*, ed. Loren Logsdon and Charles W. Mayer (Macomb, Ill.: Western Illinois University Press, 1987), 150.

15. Kathleen Westfall Shute, "Finding the Words: The Struggle for Salvation in the Fiction of Raymond Carver," *The Hollins Critic* 24, no. 5 (1987): 1; hereafter cited in the text as Shute.

16. Stewart Kellerman, "Grace Has Come into My Life," *New York Times Book Review*, 15 May 1988, 40.

17. William Stull, letter to the author, 18 February 1989.

18. *Where I'm Calling From: New and Selected Stories* (New York: Atlantic Monthly Press, 1988), 339; hereafter cited in the text as *Where*.
19. John Barth, "A Few Words about Minimalism," *New York Times Book Review*, 28 December 1986, 2.
20. Federick Barthelme, "On Being Wrong: Convicted Minimalist Spills Bean," *New York Times Book Review*, 3 April 1988, 25; hereafter cited in the text as Barthelme.

Adam Meyer

At this point in his career, there can be little doubt that Raymond Carver is "as successful as a short story writer in America can be,"[1] that "he is becoming an Influence."[2] Still, despite (or perhaps because of) this position, Carver remains a controversial figure. Much of the debate about Carver's merits centers on a similar debate about minimalism, a style that a few years ago was very hot and very hotly criticized, and that, now that it is cooling off, is under even more fervent attack. Much of the controversy is sparked by a confusion of terminology. As hard as it is accurately to define minimalism, for the same reasons we cannot entirely pin down such terms as realism, modernism, or post-modernism. It is even harder to say who is or is not a minimalist, as demonstrated by Donald Barthelme's being called a minimalist as often as he is called one of the post-modernists against whom the minimalists are rebelling.[3] Nevertheless, Carver is generally acknowledged to be "the chief practitioner of what's been called 'American minimalism.'"[4] Now that this has become a pejorative appellation, however, his admirers are quickly trying "to abduct [him] from the camp of the minimalists."[5] If he is to be successfully "abducted," however, it will not be because the label is no longer popular, but because it no longer fits.

The fact of Carver's membership in the minimalist fraternity has never been fully established. Many critics, as well as Carver himself, noted that his latest volume of new stories, *Cathedral*, seemed to be moving away from minimalist writing, that it showed a widening of perception and style.[6] This is certainly true, but it is not the whole story. If we look back over Carver's entire output, an overview en-

From "Now You See Him, Now You Don't, Now You Do Again: The Evolution of Raymond Carver's Minimalism," *Critique* 30 (1989): 239–51. © 1989 *Critique*. Reprinted by permission. The documentation has been altered to conform with that of this book.

couraged by the recent publication of his "selected" stories, *Where I'm Calling From*, we see that his career, rather than following an inverted pyramid pattern, has actually taken on the shape of an hourglass, beginning wide, then narrowing, and then widening out again. In other words, to answer the question "Is Raymond Carver a minimalist?" we must also consider the question "Which Raymond Carver are we talking about?," for he did not start out as a minimalist, and he is one no longer, although he was one for a period of time in between.

This hourglass pattern emerges when we read all of Carver's stories chronologically, or, to a lesser extent, when we read *Where I'm Calling From* from cover to cover. Carver's evolution can perhaps be best understood when we examine several stories that have been published at different times in different versions. Carver, an inveterate rewriter, has stated that he would "rather tinker with a story after writing it, and then tinker some more, changing this, changing that, than have to write the story in the first place."[7] Sometimes this tinkering results in only minor changes, as Carver makes clear when he cites admiration for Evan Connell's statement, "he knew he was finished with a short story when he found himself going through it and taking out commas and then going through the story again and putting commas back in the same places" (*Fires*, 15). At other times, however, the result is an almost entirely different work. While the rewriting process is not unusual in itself, Carver's unwillingness to stop even after a piece has been published is not typical. One significantly revised publication that has elicited much critical commentary is "A Small, Good Thing," which appears in *Cathedral*. It is a retelling of "The Bath," a story from Carver's most minimalistic volume, *What We Talk About When We Talk About Love*, that transforms the piece into something far removed from that style. In fact, this change was responsible for alerting many readers and critics to the "new" Carver presented in *Cathedral* as a whole.[8]

The basic situation in both stories is the same. A woman goes to a baker to order a special cake for her son Scotty's birthday party. The morning of his birthday, however, he is struck by a hit-and-run driver and becomes comatose. The baker, knowing only that the cake has not been picked up, calls the house and leaves threatening messages. The presentation of these events is very different in the two works, so by comparing them we can come to understand some of the salient features of minimalism. Most obviously, "The Bath," ten pages long, is approximately one-third the length of "A Small, Good Thing," an indication of the further development of the rewritten version. The characters in both stories are usually referred to by common nouns or pronouns (the boy, the mother, he, she), but in "The Bath" we do not learn the mother's full name, Ann Weiss, until the last page, whereas she announces it to the baker in the second paragraph of "A Small, Good Thing." This might seem like a small thing, but it is indicative of a larger change. If we juxtapose the two versions of this early encounter between Mrs. Weiss and the baker, we clearly see a fundamental change in Carver's narrative strategy. In "The Bath," Carver writes: "The mother decided on the spaceship cake, and then she gave the baker her name and her telephone number. The cake would be ready Monday morning, in plenty of time for the party Monday afternoon. This was all the baker was willing to say. No pleasantries, just this small exchange, the barest information, nothing that was not necessary."[9]

In "A Small, Good Thing," Carver rewrites:

> She gave the baker her name, Ann Weiss, and her telephone number. The cake would be ready on Monday morning, just out of the oven, in plenty of time for the child's party that afternoon. The baker was not jolly. There were no pleasantries between them, just the minimum exchange of words, the necessary information. He made her feel uncomfortable, and she didn't like that. While he was bent over the counter with the pencil in his hand, she studied his coarse features and wondered if he'd ever done anything else with his life besides be a baker. She was a mother and thirty-three years old, and it seemed to her that everyone, especially someone the baker's age—a man old enough to be her father—must have children who'd gone through this special time of cakes and birthday parties. There must be that between them, she thought. But he was abrupt with her—not rude, just abrupt. She gave up trying to make friends with him. She looked into the back of the bakery and could see a long, heavy wooden table with aluminum pie pans stacked at one end; and beside the table a metal container filled with empty racks. There was an enormous oven. A radio was playing country-Western music.[10]

The first version is sparse and elliptical, giving the reader only "the barest information, nothing that [is] not necessary," while the second offers a more expansive view, providing physical details of the characters and the bakery, as well as exploring the mother's thoughts. The revision also hints more fully at the conflict that will be developed later in the story. Kim Herzinger's definition of minimalism, "equanimity of surface, 'ordinary' subjects, recalcitrant narrators and deadpan narratives, slightness of story, and characters who don't think out loud,"[11] clearly fits the first paragraph, but it does not entirely account for the second, particularly in its exploration of the character's inner thoughts.

The most significant change from "The Bath" to "A Small, Good Thing," however, is in their endings. Minimalist stories have been heavily criticized for their tendency to end "with a sententious ambiguity that leaves the reader holding the bag,"[12] and "The Bath" certainly follows this pattern. It ends literally in the middle of one of the baker's telephone calls: "'Scotty,' the voice said. 'It is about Scotty,' the voice said. 'It has to do with Scotty, yes.'" (*What*, 56). At this point in the story, Scotty's medical condition is still uncertain, and, although the reader has figured it out, the parents still do not know who is making the horrible calls. This ending, then, is very much up in the air, and the reader leaves the story with a feeling of uneasiness and fear. "A Small, Good Thing," however, goes beyond this point in time. Scotty dies. The parents come to realize that the baker has been making the harassing calls, and they confront him. Once they explain the situation, the baker, feeling deep remorse for having bothered them, offers them some fresh rolls, telling them that "[e]ating is a small, good thing in a time like this" (*Cathedral*, 88). The story now ends on a note of communion, of shared understanding and grief: "They talked on into the early morning, the high, pale cast of light in the windows, and they did not think of leaving" (*Cathedral*, 89). The result is a story that has moved far beyond its minimalist origins. Carver said in an interview that "[t]he story hadn't been told originally, it had been messed around with, condensed and compressed in "The Bath" to highlight the qualities of menace that I wanted to emphasize. . . . But I still felt there was unfinished business, so in the midst of writing these other stories for *Cathedral* I went back to "The Bath" and tried to see what aspects of it needed to be enhanced, re-drawn, re-imagined. When I was done, I was amazed because it seemed so much better" (McCaffery, 69).

Most critics agree with this evaluation of "A Small, Good Thing," which won the O. Henry award as the best short story of 1983.[13] "The revision completes the original by turning the sum of its fragmentary parts into a coherent whole that has a powerful dramatic structure, a beginning, middle, and end," writes William Stull (Stull, 7), and Marc Chenetier feels that it signals "a movement away from threatening ambiguity, a working towards hope rather than horror, and the abandonment of features Carver may have come to consider akin to the narrative 'gimmicks' he has always denounced" (Chenetier, 170). Indeed, as indicated earlier, nearly all of the stories in *Cathedral* show this movement away from the "gimmicks" of minimalism.

By looking at a story that has been published in three different versions, we get a fuller picture of the whole of Carver's evolution, his movement at first toward and then away from minimalism. "So Much Water So Close to Home" first appeared (in book form) in Carver's second volume, the small press book *Furious Seasons* (1977). It was reprinted in his second "major" volume, *What We Talk About When We Talk About Love* (1981) and appeared a third time in another small press book, *Fires: Essays, Poems, Stories* (1983). Most recently, it appeared as one of the selected stories in *Where I'm Calling From* (1988). The basic plot is the same in each publication. Stuart Kane and his buddies go fishing. As soon as they arrive at their campsite, they find a dead girl floating in the river. They decide to tie her to a tree so that she will not be lost downstream and then proceed to fish and drink for the remainder of the weekend. The story is told from the point of view of Stuart's wife, Claire, and is largely concerned with the strain that this event puts on their marriage, as she, empathizing with the dead girl, feels that her husband should have abandoned his trip and reported the body immediately.

A comparison of the way this material is treated in the first and second versions shows the several ways in which, according to John Barth, a story can be minimalistic. First, Barth says, "there are minimalisms of unit, form and scale: short . . . paragraphs, super-short stories" (Barth, 8); Carver's story is reduced by half in the revision, and long paragraphs, such as the one in which Claire explains the circumstances of the body's discovery, are broken up into many smaller ones (in this case, five). Second, "there are minimalisms of style: a stripped-down vocabulary; a stripped-down syntax that avoids periodic sentences" (Barth, 8–9); this can be seen in Carver's alteration of "They fish together every spring and summer, the first two or three months of the season, before family vacations, little league baseball and visiting relatives can intrude"[14] to "They fish together every spring and early summer before visiting relatives can get in the way" (*What*, 80). Third, and most important, "there are minimalisms of material: minimal characters, minimal exposition . . . , minimal *mises en scene*, minimal action,

147

minimal plot" (Barth, 9); this third of Barth's observations is the one on which I wish to concentrate and illustrate here, for it is the key to seeing the change in Carver's aesthetic.

In the first version (*Seasons*, 1977), we are given long descriptions of the fishing trip, of Claire's reactions to her husband's behavior, of her thoughts about their past relationship, of the physical separation she imposes upon him, of the identification and subsequent funeral of the dead girl, and of many other actions and thoughts on several characters' parts. In the second version (*What*, 1981), however, these passages are either considerably reduced or eliminated altogether. As a result, this second version, since it stays on the surface of events and does not really allow us to get inside of the characters, seems to confirm the criticism that Carver's work is cold or unfeeling, that he lacks sympathy for his characters. For example, the last line of the opening paragraph in the first version—Claire's "Something has come between us though he would like to believe otherwise" (*Seasons*, 41)—sets up, even sums up, much of the emotional conflict that is to be examined in the story. Its elimination in the second version leaves us unsure of the real motivations of the characters, thus diminishing our understanding of what is actually going on and, consequently, our concern for the people involved.

There are many more examples of such revisions, excisions that require more inference on the reader's part than providing him with more information. Consider, for instance, a long passage from the first version in which Claire thinks back on her previous life:

> The past is unclear. It is as if there is a film over those early years. I cannot be sure that the things I remember happening really happened to me. There was a girl who had a mother and father—the father ran a small cafe where the mother acted as waitress and cashier—who moved as if in a dream through grade school and high school and then, in a year or two, into secretarial school. Later, much later—what happened to the time in between?—she is in another town working as a receptionist for an electronic parts firm and becomes acquainted with one of the engineers who asks her for a date. Eventually, seeing that's his aim, she lets him seduce her. . . . After a short while they decide to get married, but already the past, her past, is slipping away. The future is something she can't imagine. (*Seasons*, 49–50)

This passage, continuing in much the same vein for the rest of the page, provides us with valuable information about the character, her background, and her feelings about herself and her marriage. Therefore, when this is replaced by "I sit for a long time holding the newspaper and thinking" (*What*, 84), we are obviously missing out on a key to understanding the actions within the story. We also miss out on fully comprehending the developing relationship between Stuart and Claire when several scenes showing her physical revulsion toward her husband, the way "his fingers burn" (*Seasons*, 51) when he touches her, are reduced or eliminated. A long argument about her refusing to sleep in the same bed with him (*Seasons*, 53), for example, becomes "That night I make my bed on the sofa" (*What*, 85), again making it harder for the reader to grasp what is going on in the story. Unlike the first version, these elliptical revisions result in a minimalistic story whose "prose [is] so attenuated that it can't support the weight of a past or a future, but only a bare notation of what happens, now; a slice of life in which the characters are seen without the benefit of antecedents or social context" (Gorra, 155).

Not only does the first version provide a fuller understanding of the main characters, it also presents important and detailed pictures of some of the minor characters who are all but eliminated in the revision. We have already seen how the baker's transformation from a mere voice on the other end of the telephone in "The Bath" to a fully realized person with his own history and concerns in "A Small, Good Thing" adds a whole new dimension, a fuller sense of humanity to that story, and the same is true here. For example, Carver's revision of "So Much Water So Close to Home" eliminates an important scene in which the couple's son, Dean, questions his father, only to be told to be quiet by his mother (*Seasons*, 51). More significantly, Carver dramatically redraws his portrait of the victim. Although it seems like a minor detail, there is a world of difference in the reader's perception when a character is called "Susan Miller" rather than "the body." The *Furious Seasons* version of "So Much Water So Close to Home" contains the following scene, a description of a television news report in which the dead girl's parents go into the funeral home to identify the body: "Bewildered, sad, they shuffle slowly up the sidewalk to the front steps to where a man in a dark suit stands waiting and holding the door. Then, it seems as if only a second has passed, as if they have merely gone inside the door and turned around and come out again, the same couple is shown leaving the mortuary, the woman in tears, covering her face with a handkerchief, the man stopping long enough to say to a reporter, 'It's her, it's Susan'" (*Seasons*, 52).

There is also a description of what she looked like, her high school graduation picture flashed on the screen, and what she did for a living. In this way, she and her family become alive for the reader, who is now able to identify with them just as Claire does. When all we are told is that "the body has been identified, claimed" (*What*, 84), however, we fail to reach this sort of understanding. We also therefore fail to understand fully Claire's motivation in attending her funeral.

Once again, the ending has been radically changed in the rewrite. In the first version, Claire returns from the funeral. Stuart attempts to initiate physical contact with her, but she rebuffs him, even stomping on his foot. He throws her down, makes an obscene remark, and goes away for the night. He sends her flowers the next morning, attempting to make up, but she "move[s her] things into the extra bedroom" (*Seasons*, 60). At the end of the story, still not understanding his actions, she says to him, "'For God's sake, Stuart, she was only a child'" (*Seasons*, 61). Her sense of continued sympathy for Susan and incomprehension of Stuart's behavior, her further separation from him, is perfectly in keeping with the previous actions and motivations of the characters. She had said earlier that her real fear was that "one day something [would] happen that should change something, but then you see nothing is going to change after all" (*Seasons*, 49), yet it is clear at the end of the story that a fundamental alteration of her marital relationship has occurred. In the second version of the story, however, when Stuart attempts to initiate sexual activity with her, she allows herself to be symbolically raped; the sentence "I can't hear a thing with so much water going" (*What*, 88) clearly recalls the rape and murder of the other girl. She even goes so far as to participate actively in the violation. "'That's right,' I say, finishing the buttons myself. 'Before Dean comes. Hurry'" (*What*, 88). Her motivation here is unclear, made even more so by its having been so understated in the earlier parts of the story. We do not understand what has caused her to change her mind about Stuart, nor why she is seemingly willing to return to the status quo. The ending is not ambiguous, like the ending of "The Bath," but it is rather illogical and unconvincingly forced.

As we have seen, then, the revision of this story makes it more minimal than it had been, reduces it rather than enlarges it. When Carver assembled the stories for *Fires*, however, he decided to republish the first version (with some minor changes) rather than the second. As he explains in the afterword to the volume, "I decided to stay fairly close to the versions as they first appeared . . . , which is more in accord with the way I am writing stories these days [i.e., the stories in *Cathedral*]" (*Fires*, 189).[15] Elsewhere Carver has stated that *What We Talk About When We Talk About Love* is a very "self-conscious book in the sense of how intentional every move was, how calculated. I pushed and pulled and worked with those stories before they went into the book to an extent I'd never done with any other stories" (Simpson, 316). The end result, however, was not entirely satisfactory. "I knew I'd gone as far the other way as I could or wanted to go," he said, "cutting everything down to the marrow, not just to the bone" (Simpson, 317), so he began to move in the other direction, first in *Fires* and then in *Cathedral*. Carver's movement away from minimalism is also apparent in his selection of the stories to be included in *Where I'm Calling From*. Only seven of the seventeen stories in *What We Talk About When We Talk About Love* are included, compared with eight of the twelve in *Cathedral*. Even more tellingly, Carver chooses four stories that appear "minimalized" in *What We Talk About When We Talk About Love* but reprints them in their other, fuller forms—for example, "A Small, Good Thing" rather than "The Bath" and the third "So Much Water So Close to Home" rather than the second.

This movement at first toward but then away from minimalism can also be traced in "Distance," otherwise known as "Everything Stuck to Him" (in *What*), another story that is printed in all four volumes *(Seasons, What, Fires, Where)*. While the changes here are much less dramatic than those in the three versions of "So Much Water So Close to Home," the pattern is similar. The location of the story, for instance, is given in the first version as "Milan . . . in his apartment in the Via Fabroni near the Cascina Gardens" (*Seasons*, 27), in the second as simply "Milan" (*What*, 127), and in the third as "Milan . . . in his apartment on the Via Fabroni near the Cascina Gardens" (*Fires*, 113). The lack of specificity in the second version indicates that it has been "minimalized," but Carver ultimately rejects this in favor of the fuller, more detailed description.[16] The story is selected for *Where I'm Calling From* in this third version.

An even better example of these changes in Carver's aesthetic, however, is the story "Where Is Everyone?," which was first published in the journal *TriQuarterly* in the spring of 1980. It reappeared, under the title "Mr. Coffee and Mr. Fixit," in *What We Talk About When We Talk*

About Love (1981). In the transition it was reduced by a third, Carver having cut from it the same sort of material that he excised in the second publication of "So Much Water So Close to Home." The story does not have much of a plot in either case. It is rather unusual among Carver's stories in that it is almost entirely composed of the narrator's reminiscences of past events, such as his wife's affair with an unemployed aerospace worker, his children and their actions, his father's death, and his widowed mother's sexual activities. The story is difficult to follow both chronologically and emotionally in both versions, but in the earlier, fuller version we are given many more clues. As Marc Chenetier points out, "in its much longer version as "Where Is Everyone?," it makes plain a number of details that remain quite puzzling in the shortened text. . . . The barest skeleton necessary for suggestion remains and a number of incidents that can be read as explanation in "Where Is Everyone?" are left as mere questions or unclear allusions in "Mr. Coffee and Mr. Fixit." . . . All of the details that made for "understanding" or "answering" a story in the interrogative mode have been toned down and have lodged the interrogations dismissed from the title at the heart of the story itself" (Chenetier, 179).

The two stories begin similarly, but they diverge sharply in a passage in which the narrator recalls his relationship with his children. "I hated my kids during this time," he says. "One afternoon I got into a scuffle with my son. . . . I said I would kill him."[17] He goes on to explain the way the children, Katy and Mike, tried to take advantage of the situation, but he indicates that they were also deeply hurt by it, as seen by Mike's locking his mother out of the house one morning after she had spent the night at her lover's house and then beating her up when he does let her in. Not only is this passage missing from the revised version, but the son has been eliminated from the story altogether, and the daughter, whose name has been changed from Katy to Melody, just as the wife's has gone from Cynthia to Myrna, is little more than a stick figure who only appears in one brief paragraph. The result again is to provide the reader with less information about the state of the family; we get hints, but that is all. The narrator is also more reticent about himself. His comparing the situation to a scene in a novel by Italo Svevo (*TQ*, 206), for instance, provides some insight into his personality and sets him apart from the standard, even stereotypical, Carver character. Not only does he read, a rarity in itself, but he reads novels by obscure Italian writers. This reference is eliminated in the revision, once more depriving us of a fact that might help us to make sense of the character's actions. The same is true of the sentence "'No one's evil,' I said once to Cynthia when we were discussing my own affair" (*TQ*, 210). This fact, as well as the way it seems to slip out without the narrator's being fully aware of having divulged it, opens up a whole new level of interest and awareness, one that remains blocked off when the line is deleted, as it is in the second version.

This obscuring of the central characters and their relationships continues throughout "Mr. Coffee and Mr. Fixit." In "Where Is Everyone?," although the narrator says that "conversations touching on love or the past were rare" (*TQ*, 208), they do exist and are presented to us. At one point, for example, Cynthia says to the narrator, "When I was pregnant with Mike you carried me into the bathroom when I was so sick and pregnant I couldn't get out of bed. You carried me. No one else will ever do that, no one else could ever love me in that way, that much. We have that, no matter what. We've loved each other like nobody else could or ever will love the other again" (*TQ*, 207). This glimpse of the past, besides being touching, appearing as it does in the midst of anger and violence, explains the tie that binds the couple together despite their problems. Ironically, the other important interpersonal relationship in the story exists between the narrator and his wife's lover, Ross, even though they have never met. In "Mr. Coffee and Mr. Fixit," there are a few elliptical references to this feeling of connection on the narrator's part: "But we had things in common, Ross and me, which was more than just the same woman" (*What*, 19); or "I used to make fun of him when I had the chance. But I don't make fun of him anymore. God bless you and keep you, Mr. Fixit" (*What*, 19–20). The rationale behind these statements is obscure. Here is another example of a peculiar bind that Carver can get himself into; when he "omit[s] what other writers might regard as essential information, it is often hard to know what has precipitated a given situation."[18] In "Where Is Everyone?," these passages are expanded, and the connection becomes easier to see. For example, the narrator had once suggested that Mike join the Army. Cynthia disagreed, but Ross spoke in favor of the idea. "I was pleased to hear this," the narrator says, "and to find out that Ross and I were in agreement on the matter. Ross went up a peg in my estimation. . . . He [had] told her this even after there'd been a pushing and shoving match out in his drive in the early morning hours when Mike had thrown him down on the pavement" (*TQ*, 208). The narrator was more than willing to admit to his wife that Ross was "[o]ne of *us*" (*TQ*, 210) at the time, and now he realizes that his anger toward Ross was really only jealousy because "he was something of a fallen hero to my kids and to Cynthia, too, I suppose, because he'd helped put men on the moon" (*TQ*, 209). In the longer version, then, Ross, like the minor characters we have examined in the other stories, emerges as a person in his own right, more than just the lover of the narrator's wife. We can now see how the narrator comes to identify with him (they are, after all, two men in similar positions) and eventually to forgive him. When all we see is the forgiveness, though, we do not understand how it came to be.

Once again the endings are significantly different from one version to the other. In "Where Is Everyone?," the narrator returns to his mother's house to spend the night. She reluctantly informs him of his wife's affair. He tells her, "I know that. . . . His name is Ross and he's an alcoholic. He's like me" (*TQ*, 212). She responds, "Honey, you're going to have to do something for yourself" (*TQ*, 212) and wishes him good night. The story ends with the following description: "I lay there staring at the TV. There were images of uniformed men on the screen, a low murmur, then tanks and a man using a flame thrower. I couldn't hear it, but I didn't want to get up. I kept staring until I felt my eyes close. But I woke up with a start, the pajamas damp with sweat. A snowy light filled the room. There was a roaring coming at me. The room clamored. I lay there. I didn't move" (*TQ*, 213). This ending is somewhat ambiguous, but it does point to an apocalyptic change in the narrator's life, the sort that has resulted in his having reached the level of understanding he possesses at the time, about three years later, when he is narrating these events. "Mr. Coffee and Mr. Fixit," however, ends in this manner:

> "Honey," I said to Myrna the night she came home. "Let's hug awhile and then you fix us a real nice supper."
> Myrna said, "Wash your hands." (*What*, 20)

This ending so lacks any kind of summation, let alone consummation, that it baffles the reader. We do not even know when "the night she came home" is—Is it at the time of the events or at the time of their narration? What will be the effect of the things of which we have been told on the lives of those involved? We simply have to guess, with little to go on. Once asked about his endings, Carver stated, "I want to make sure my readers aren't left feeling cheated in one way or another when they've finished my stories. It's important for writers to provide enough to satisfy readers, even if they don't provide 'the' answers, or clear resolutions" (McCaffery, 78). The ending of "Mr. Coffee and Mr. Fixit," however, far from being satisfying, is the sort that "rather than suggest[ing] depth . . . only signal[s] authorial cop out."[19] This is undoubtedly one of the reasons that, as in the case of "So Much Water So Close to Home," when Carver compiled the material for *Fires*, he returned, nearly word for word, to the original fuller version. Still one of his less successful pieces, as he tacitly admits by not selecting it for *Where I'm Calling From*, "Where Is Everyone?" is certainly better in that less minimal form.

John Biguenet finds "Mr. Coffee and Mr. Fixit" to be such a good example of everything he dislikes about minimalism that he uses it as the principal illustration in his satirical article "Notes of a Disaffected Reader: The Origins of Minimalism." After providing a summary of the story that is almost as long as the story itself, he writes: "It sounds like parody, doesn't it? Fifteen years ago it would have been parody. But it's not parody; it's paraphrase. If paraphrase is literature purged of style, then paraphrase is a kind of minimalism, and since the absence of style is a style itself, a disaffected reader might argue that paraphrase is an apt description of minimalist style. The reader, like a child with crayons hunched over a coloring book, authors the story."[20] In "Where Is Everyone?," however, Carver has already colored in the story for us, and we must keep in mind that it is this fuller, more expansive, more "authorly" version that he ultimately chooses to stand by. As we have seen by comparing the three versions of this story, as well as the various versions of other stories we have examined, Carver has undergone an aesthetic evolution, at first moving toward minimalism but then turning sharply away from it. The stories in *What We Talk About When We Talk About Love,* including "The Bath," the second "So Much Water So Close to Home," and "Mr. Coffee and Mr. Fixit," do indeed follow Barth's definition of the "minimalist esthetic, of which a cardinal principle is that artistic effect may be enhanced by a radical economy of artistic means, even where such parsimony compromises other values: completeness, for example, or richness or precision of statement" (Barth, 5). In the final analysis, however, Carver rejects this minimalist aesthetic. In *Fires* and *Cathedral,* and in the selected (and, incidentally, the new) stories in *Where I'm Calling From*, he is clearly opting for "completeness, richness, and precision." Therefore, if "most readers [take] their measure of him from his second collection of stories [i.e., *What*]" (Stull, 1), they get a distorted picture of the actual scope and direction of his writings, which "both before and since" (Stull, 2) that volume are quite different.[21] Carver has said that he does not consider himself a minimalist, that "there's something about minimalist that smacks of smallness of vision and execution that I don't like" (Simpson, 317), but this statement alone is not enough to remove the label. What should be enough, however, is the content of the work itself; rather than simply expressing his dissatisfaction with those stories he felt "were becoming too attenuated" (McCaffery, 65), he rewrote them or returned to an earlier version of them, so that they were more in keeping with his real style. It is no coincidence that, as he has moved away from his archminimalist phase to a more natural form, he has no longer felt this need to rewrite. "I feel that the stories in *Cathedral* are finished in a way I rarely felt about my stories previously," he told an interviewer shortly after the publication of that volume (McCaffery, 67), and in a profile written at the time of the publication of *Where I'm Calling From*, he expresses regret at having "mutilated" some of his earlier stories when he says, "I used to revise even after a story was printed. I guess now I have a little more confidence."[22] As this most recent collection makes abundantly clear, Raymond Carver may have been a minimalist, but he used to be and has once again become much more.

Notes

1. Mark Facknitz, "'The Calm,' 'A Small, Good Thing,' and 'Cathedral': Raymond Carver and the Recovery of Human Worth," *Studies in Short Fiction* 23, no. 3 (1986): 287.

2. Robert Houston, "A Stunning Inarticulateness," *Nation*, 4 July 1981, 23.

3. The best discussion of these issues is found in the special "Minimalism" edition of *Mississippi Review* 40–41 (Winter 1985): 7–22. The essays are edited by Kim A. Herzinger, who also contributes a fine introduction setting forth the problems of definition and inclusion. Several of the other essays are quite useful (and often humorous), and an important interview with Carver is included. Nor should one miss John Barth's excellent "A Few Words about Minimalism," *Weber Studies* 4 (1987): 5–14, the most succinct and enlightening view of the controversy yet to appear; hereafter cited in the text as Barth.

4. Michael Gorra, "Laughter and Bloodshed," *Hudson Review* 37 (Spring 1984): 155; hereafter cited in the text as Gorra.

5. Marilynne Robinson, "Marriage and Other Astonishing Bonds," *New*

York Times Book Review, 15 May 1988, 1. It is interesting to note that Robinson herself is often grouped with the minimalists.

6. Carver's comments can be found in his interviews with Mona Simpson and Lewis Buzbee, *Writers at Work: The Paris Review Interviews*, seventh series, ed. George Plimpton (New York: Viking, 1986): 317–18; hereafter cited in the text as Simpson; Larry McCaffery and Sinda Gregory, *Mississippi Review* 40–41 (1985): 65; hereafter cited in the text as McCaffery; and Kay Bonetti, *Saturday Review* 9 (September–October 1983): 22. Critics who have made remarks along these lines include Anatole Broyard, "Diffuse Regrets," *New York Times*, 5 September 1983, 27; Irving Howe, "Stories of Our Loneliness," *New York Times Book Review*, 11 September 1983, 1, 43; Laurie Stone, "Feeling No Pain," *Voice Literary Supplement* 20 (October 1983): 55; Bruce Allen, "MacArthur Award Winners Produce Two of Season's Best," *The Christian Science Monitor*, 4 November 1983, B4; Dorothy Wickendon, "Old Darkness, New Light," *New Republic*, 21 November 1983, 38; Josh Rubins, "Small Expectations," *New York Review of Books*, 24 November 1983, 41–42; and Michael J. Bugeja, "Tarnish and Silver: An Analysis of Carver's *Cathedral*," *South Dakota Review* 24, no. 3 (Autumn 1986): 73, 82–83, 87.

7. *Fires: Essays, Poems, Stories* (Santa Barbara, Calif: Capra Press, 1983), 188; further references will be parenthetical (*Fires*).

8. The most useful account of these two stories is in the best single article on Carver, William Stull's, "Beyond Hopelessville: Another Side of Raymond Carver," *Philological Quarterly* 64, no. 1 (Winter 1985): 1–15; hereafter cited in the text as Stull. I have kept my comments about them brief here largely because of his excellent explication. Other critics who touch on "The Bath" and "A Small, Good Thing" include Howe, 43; Allen, B4; Rubins 41–42; Jonathan Yardley, "Ordinary People from an Extraordinary Writer," *Washington Post Book World*, 4 September 1983, 3; and Marc Chenetier, "Living On/ Off the 'Reserve': Performance, Interrogation, and Negativity in the Works of Raymond Carver," in *Critical Angles: European Views of Contemporary American Literature*, ed. Marc Chenetier (Carbondale, Ill.: Southern Illinois University Press, 1986), 170; hereafter cited in the text as Chenetier. Carver himself remarks on these two stories in his interview with McCaffery and Gregory, 66.

9. *What We Talk about When We Talk about Love* (New York: Alfred A. Knopf, 1981), 48; further references will be parenthetical (*What*).

10. *Cathedral* (New York: Alfred A. Knopf, 1983), 80; further references will be parenthetical (*Cathedral*).

11. Kim A. Herzinger, "Introduction: On the New Fiction," *Mississippi Review* 40–41 (Winter 1985): 7.

12. Anatole Broyard, "Books of the Times," *New York Times*, 15 April 1981, C29. For other criticisms of Carver's minimalist endings see Gorra, 156; Stull, 2, 5; and Adam Mars-Jones, "Words for the Walking Wounded," *Times Literary Supplement*, 22 January 1982, 76.

13. William Abrahams, ed., *Prize Stories 1983: The O. Henry Awards* (Garden City, N.Y.: Doubleday, 1983). Abrahams has a brief paragraph in his introduction explaining why he so much prefers "A Small, Good Thing" to "The Bath." A dissenting view, however, can be seen in Rubins, 41–42, who finds the new ending too sentimental.

14. *Furious Seasons* (Santa Barbara, Calif.: Capra Press, 1977), 43; further references will be parenthetical (*Seasons*).

15. Carver also comments on the different versions of this story in his interview with Kay Bonetti, which is available on cassette through the American Audio Prose Library (CV III 1083). The excerpt from the interview that appears in *Saturday Review* does not include this portion.

16. Chenetier briefly discusses the story's three versions, but he misses this all-important point when he states that "Distance" is "retitled 'Everything Stuck to Him' in its passage from *Fires* and *Furious Seasons* to *What We Talk About*" (176). The correct chronology is from *Furious Seasons* to *What We Talk About* and then back to *Fires*, thus conforming to the hourglass pattern I have been stressing.

17. "Where Is Everyone?" *TriQuarterly* 48 (Spring 1980): 203; further references will be parenthetical (*TQ*).

18. Robert Towers, "Low Rent Tragedies," *New York Review of Books*, 14 May 1981, 37.

19. Peter LaSalle, untitled review, *America*, 30 January 1982, 80.

20. John Biguenet, "Notes of a Disaffected Reader: The Origins of Minimalism," *Mississippi Review* 40–41 (1985): 44.

21. See also Stull, 6, 14n. Stull is the only critic to have remarked on this "before and since" pattern that I have been exploring, but he does so only in passing.

22. David Gates, "Carver: To Make a Long Story Short," *Newsweek*, 6 June 1988, 70.

Chronology

1938   Raymond Carver born 25 May, to Clevie Raymond and Ella Casey Carver in Clatskanie, Oregon.

1941   Family moves to Yakima, Washington.

1957   Marries Maryann Burk on 7 June. Daughter, Christine LaRae, born 2 December.

1958   Family moves to Paradise, California. Carver enters Chico State College. Son, Vance Lindsay, born 17 October.

1959   Enrolls in John Gardner's creative writing course.

1960   Transfers to Humbolt State College.

1962   "Pastoral" accepted for publication by *Western Humanities Review*.

1963   Graduates with A. B. from Humbolt State College (now California State University, Humbolt). *Western Humanities Review* publishes "Pastoral." Enters Iowa Writers Workshop.

1964   Leaves the program without completing the academic year.

1966   *December* publishes "Will You Please Be Quiet, Please?"

1967   "Will You Please Be Quiet, Please?" anthologized in *Best American Short Stories*. Takes job editing textbooks for Science Research Associates, Palo Alto, California.

1968   *Near Klamath* (poems) published by Sacramento State College.

1970   *Winter Insomnia* (poems) published by Kayak Press. Loses job at Science Research Associates. Receives National Endowment for the Arts Discovery Award for Poetry. "Sixty Acres" reprinted in *Best Little Magazine Fiction*. "Will You Please Be Quiet, Please?" anthologized in *Short Stories from the Literary Magazines*.

1971   Lectures at University of California, Santa Cruz. *Esquire* publishes "Neighbors." "A Night Out" reprinted in *Best Little Magazine Fiction*.

1972   Receives Wallace Stegner Creative Writing Fellowship, Stanford University. Lectures at University of California, Berkeley. Receives Joseph Henry Jackson Award for Fiction.

1973   Lectures at Iowa Writers Workshop. "What Is It?" reprinted in *Prize Stories, 1973: The O. Henry Awards.*

1974   *Put Yourself in My Shoes* (chapbook) published by Capra Press. "Put Yourself in My Shoes" in *Prize Stories, 1974: The O. Henry Awards.*

1975   "Are You a Doctor?" in *Prize Stories, 1975: The O. Henry Awards.*

1976   *Will You Please Be Quiet, Please?* (stories) published by McGraw-Hill. *At Night the Salmon Move* (poems) published by Capra Press. "So Much Water So Close to Home" included in *Pushcart Prize: The Best of the Small Presses.*

1977   Awarded Guggenheim Fellowship. *Will You Please Be Quiet, Please?* nominated for National Book Award. Separates from Maryann Carver. *Furious Seasons and Other Stories* published by Capra Press.

1978   Visiting Distinguished Writer, University of Texas at El Paso. Meets Tess Gallagher.

1979   National Endowment for the Arts Fellowship for Fiction.

1980   Professor of English, Syracuse University.

1981   *What We Talk about When We Talk about Love* published by Alfred A. Knopf. "What We Talk about When We Talk about Love" included in *Pushcart Prize Anthology.*

1982   Divorces Maryann Carver. "Cathedral" included in *Best American Short Stories* and *Pushcart Prize Anthology.* Quits drinking. *Two Poems* published by Scarab Press.

1983   *Cathedral* published by Alfred A. Knopf. "Where I'm Calling From" included in *Best American Short Stories.* "A Small, Good Thing" in *Prize Stories, 1983: The O. Henry Awards* and *Pushcart Prize.* *Cathedral* nominated for National Book Critics Circle Award and Pulitzer Prize. Carver receives a Mildred and Harold Strauss Living Award. *Fires: Essays, Poems, Stories* published by Capra Press. Resigns professorship at Syracuse.

1984   *If It Please You* (poems) published by Lord John. "Careful" selected for *Pushcart Prize.*

1985   *Where Water Comes Together with Other Water* (poems) published by Random House. *This Water* (poems) published by Ewert.

Awarded Levinson Prize. *Dostoevsky: A Screenplay*, with Tess Gallagher, published by Capra Press. *The Stories of Raymond Carver* published by Picador Press.

1986   *Ultramarine* (poems) published by Random House.

1988   Carver marries Tess Gallagher in June. *Where I'm Calling From* published by Atlantic Monthly Press. Elected to the American Academy and Institute of Arts and Letters. "Errand," first prize in *Prize Stories, 1988: The O. Henry Awards*, also anthologized in *Best American Short Stories, 1988*. Dies from lung cancer in Port Angeles, Washington, 2 August.

1989   *A New Path to the Waterfall* (poems) published by Atlantic Monthly Press.

Selected Bibliography

Primary Sources

Collections

Cathedral. New York: Alfred A. Knopf, 1983. Includes "Feathers," "Chef's House," "Preservation," "The Compartment," "A Small, Good Thing," "Vitamins," "Careful," "Where I'm Calling From," "The Train," "Fever," "The Bridle," "Cathedral."

Fires: Essays, Poems, Stories. Santa Barbara, Calif.: Capra Press, 1983. Includes "Distance," "The Lie," "The Cabin," "Harry's Death," "The Pheasant," "Where Is Everyone?" "So Much Water So Close to Home."

Furious Seasons and Other Stories. Santa Barbara, Calif.: Capra Press, 1977. Includes "Dummy," "Distance," "The Lie," "So Much Water So Close to Home," "The Fling," "Pastoral," "Mine," "Furious Seasons."

What We Talk about When We Talk about Love. New York: Alfred A. Knopf, 1981. Includes "Why Don't You Dance?" "Viewfinder," "Mr. Coffee and Mr. Fixit," "Gazebo," "I Could See the Smallest Things," "Sacks," "The Bath," "Tell the Women We're Coming," "After the Denim," "So Much Water So Close to Home," "The Third Thing That Killed My Father Off," "A Serious Talk," "The Calm," "Popular Mechanics," "Everything Stuck to Him," "What We Talk about When We Talk about Love," "One More Thing."

Where I'm Calling From: New and Selected Stories. New York: Atlantic Monthly Press, 1988. Includes "Nobody Said Anything," "Bicycles, Muscles, Cigarettes," "The Student's Wife," "They're Not Your Husband," "What Do You Do in San Francisco?" "Fat," "What's in Alaska?" "Neighbors," "Put Yourself in My Shoes," "Collectors," "Why, Honey?" "Are These Actual Miles?" "Gazebo," "One More Thing," "Little Things," "Why Don't You Dance?" "A Serious Talk," "What We Talk about When We Talk about Love," "Distance," "The Third Thing That Killed My Father Off," "So Much Water So Close to Home," "The Calm," "Vitamins," "Careful," "Where I'm Calling From," "Chef's House," "Fever," "Feathers," "Cathedral," "A Small, Good Thing," "Boxes," "Whoever Was Using This Bed," "Intimacy," "Menudo," "Elephant," "Blackbird Pie," "Errand."

Will You Please Be Quiet, Please? The Stories of Raymond Carver. New York: McGraw-Hill Book Company, 1976. Includes "Fat," "Neighbors," "The

Idea," "They're Not Your Husband," "Are You a Doctor?" "The Father," "Nobody Said Anything," "Sixty Acres," "What's in Alaska?" "Night School," "Collectors," "What Do You Do in San Francisco?" "The Student's Wife," "Put Yourself in My Shoes," "Jerry and Molly and Sam," "Why, Honey?" "The Ducks," "How about This?" "Bicycles, Muscles, Cigarets," "What Is It?" "Signals," "Will You Please Be Quiet, Please?"

Reprints in Anthologies

"After the Denim." In *Full Measure: Modern Short Stories on Aging,* ed. Dorothy Sennett, 290–99. Saint Paul, Minn.: Graywolf, 1980.

"Are You a Doctor?" In *Prize Stories, 1975: The O. Henry Awards,* ed. William Abrahams, 111–18. Garden City, N.J.: Doubleday, 1975; and *Prize Stories of the Seventies: From the O. Henry Awards,* ed. William Abrahams, 205–12. Garden City, N.J.: Doubleday, 1981.

"Boxes." In *The Bread Loaf Anthology of Contemporary American Short Stories,* ed. Robert Pack and Jay Parini, 42–56. Hanover, N.H.: University Press of New England, 1987; *The Best American Short Stories,* ed. Ann Beattie and Shannon Ravenel. Boston: Houghton Mifflin, 1987; and *New American Short Stories,* ed. Gloria Norris. New York: New American Library, 1987.

"The Calm." In *Matters of Life and Death: New American Stories,* ed. Tobias Wolff, 15–19. Green Harbor, Mass.: Wampeter Press, 1983.

"Careful." In *The Pushcart Prize Anthology: The Best of the Small Presses,* ed. Bill Henderson, 306–16. Wainscott, N.Y.: Pushcart Press, 1984.

"Cathedral." In *The Best American Short Stories, 1982,* ed. John Gardner and Shannon Ravenel, 317. Boston: Houghton Mifflin, 1982; *The Random Review,* ed. Gary Fisketjon and Jonathan Galassi, 83–101. New York: Random House, 1982; *Look Who's Talking: An Anthology of Voices in the Modern American Short Story,* ed. Bruce Weber. New York: Washington Square Press, 1986; *Writing Fiction: A Guide to Narrative Craft,* 2d ed., ed. Janet Burroway, 368–80. Glenview, Ill.: Scott, Foresman and Company, 1987; *Story: Fictions Past and Present,* ed. Boyd Litzinger and Joyce Carol Oates, 905–14. Lexington, Mass.: D. C. Heath and Company, 1985; and *Fiction 100: An Anthology of Short Stories,* 5th ed., ed. James H. Pickering, 165–74. New York: Macmillan Publishing Company, 1988.

"Errand." First Prize in *Prize Stories, 1988: The O. Henry Awards,* ed. William Abrahams, 1–13. Garden City, N.J.: Doubleday, 1988; and *The Best American Short Stories, 1988,* ed. Mark Helprin and Shannon Ravenel, 132–44. Boston: Houghton Mifflin, 1988.

"Fat." In *The Art of the Tale: An International Anthology of Short Stories, 1945–1985,* ed. Daniel Halpern, 197–200. New York: Viking, 1986.

"Fever." In *American Short Story Masterpieces,* ed. Raymond Carver and Tom Jenks. New York: Delacorte Press, 1987.

"Gazebo." In *Buying Time: An Anthology Celebrating Twenty Years of the Literature Program of the National Endowment for the Arts,* ed. Scott Walker. Saint Paul, Minn.: Graywolf Press, 1985.

"Neighbors." In *Last Night's Stranger: One Night Stands and Other Staples of Modern Life,* ed. Patricia Rotter, 26–32. New York: A&W Publishers, 1982; *The Secret Life of Our Times: New Fiction from "Esquire,"* ed. Gordon Lish, 33–41. Garden City, N.J.: Doubleday, 1973; and *Great "Esquire" Fiction: The Finest Stories from the First Fifty Years,* ed. Rust Hills. New York: Viking Press, 1983.

"A Night Out." In *The Best Little Magazine Fiction,* ed. Curt Johnson and Alvin Greenberg, 67–74. New York: New York University Press, 1970; and *Editor's Choice: Literature and Graphics from the U.S. Small Press, 1965–1977,* ed. Morty Sklar and Jim Mulac, 225–31. Iowa City, Iowa: The Spirit That Moves Us Press, 1980.

"Popular Mechanics." In *Sudden Fiction: American Short-Short Stories,* ed. Robert Shapard and James Thomas, 68–69. Salt Lake City, Utah: Gibbs M. Smith, 1986.

"Put Yourself in My Shoes." In *Prize Stories, 1974: The O. Henry Awards,* ed. William Abrahams, 215–28. Garden City, N.J.: Doubleday, 1974.

"A Small, Good Thing." First Prize in *Prize Stories, 1983: The O. Henry Awards,* ed. William Abrahams, 1–25. Garden City, N.J.: Doubleday, 1983; and in *The Ploughshares Reader: New Fiction for the Eighties,* ed. DeWitt Henry, 69–96. Wainscott, N.Y.: Pushcart Press, 1985; *The Pushcart Prize Anthology: The Best of the Small Presses,* ed. Bill Henderson. Wainscott, N.Y.: Pushcart Press, 1983; *The World of the Short Story: A Twentieth Century Collection,* ed. Clifton Fadiman, 786–805. Boston: Houghton Mifflin, 1986; and *To Read Fiction,* ed. Donald Hall, 242–57. New York: Holt, Rinehart and Winston, 1987.

"So Much Water So Close to Home." In *The Pushcart Prize Anthology: The Best of the Small Presses,* ed. Bill Henderson, 50–68. Yonkers, N.Y.: Pushcart Press, 1976.

"Viewfinder." In *A Reader of New American Fiction,* ed. Robert Fromberg and Rebecca Best. Peoria, Ill.: I-74 Press, 1981.

"What Is It?" In *Prize Stories, 1973: The O. Henry Awards,* ed. William Abrahams, 147–55. Garden City, N.J.: Doubleday, 1973.

"What We Talk about When We Talk about Love." In *The Pushcart Prize Anthology: The Best of the Small Presses,* ed. Bill Henderson, 88–100. Wainscott, N.Y.: Pushcart Press, 1981; and *The Norton Book of American Short Stories,* ed. Peter S. Prescott, 651–61. New York: W. W. Norton, 1988.

"Where I'm Calling From." In *The Best American Short Stories, 1983,* ed. Anne Tyler and Shannon Ravenel, 68–83. Boston: Houghton Mifflin, 1983; and *The Norton Anthology of Short Fiction,* 4th ed., ed. R. V. Cassill, 158–70. New York: W. W. Norton, 1990.

"Where Is Everyone?" In *TriQuarterly Twentieth Anniversary*, ed. Reginald Gibbons and Susan Hahn, 397–406. Wainscott, N.Y.: Pushcart Press, 1985.

"Why Don't You Dance?" In *Stories about How Things Fall Apart and What's Left When They Do*, ed. Allen Woodman, 51–57. Tallahassee, Fla.: Word Beat Press, 1985.

"Will You Please Be Quiet, Please?" In *The Best American Short Stories, 1967* ed. Martha Foley, 37–65. Boston: Houghton Mifflin, 1967; and *Short Stories from the Little Magazines*, ed. Jarvis Thurston and Curt Johnson, 26–46. Glenview, Ill.: Scott, Foresman and Company, 1970.

Poetry Collections

At Night the Salmon Move. Santa Barbara, Calif.: Capra Press, 1976.

If It Please You. Nortridge, Calif.: Lord John, 1984.

Near Klamath. Sacramento, Calif.: Sacramento State College, 1968.

This Water. New York: Ewert, 1985.

Two Poems. Orinda, Calif.: Scarab Press, 1982.

Ultramarine. New York: Random House, 1986.

Where Water Comes Together with Other Water. New York: Random House, 1985.

Winter Insomnia. Santa Barbara, Calif.: Kayak Press, 1970.

Screenplay

Dostoevsky: The Screenplay. With Tess Gallagher. Santa Barbara, Calif.: Capra Press, 1985.

Secondary Sources

Interviews

Baker, Tim, and Marc Heberden. "The Stories of Raymond Carver." *Paris Free Voice*, May 1987, 1, 5–6.

Bonetti, Kay. "Ray Carver: Keeping It Short." *Saturday Review* (September-October 1983): 21–23.

———. "Raymond Carver Talks about His Life." Sound cassette. Columbia, MO: AAPL, 1982.

———. "Interview with Raymond Carver." Sound cassette. Columbia, MO: AAPL, 1983.

McCaffery, Larry, and Sinda Gregory. "An Interview with Raymond Carver."

In *Alive and Writing*, edited by Larry McCaffery and Sinda Gregory. Urbana, Ill.: University of Illinois Press, 1987.

McElhinny, Lisa. "Raymond Carver Speaking." *Akros Review* 8–9 (Spring 1984): 103–14.

Phillips, Cassandra. "Accolade-Winning Author Returns to Humbolt." *Eureka* [Calif.] *Times-Standard*, 24 June 1977, 1–2.

Simpson, Mona, and Lewis Buzbee. "The *Paris Review* Interview." In *Fires*, 187–216. New York: Vintage Books, 1984.

Books and Parts of Books

Chenetier, Marc. "Living On/Off the 'Reserve': Performance, Interrogation, and Negativity in the Works of Raymond Carver." In *Critical Angles: European Views of Contemporary American Literature*, edited by Marc Chenetier. Carbondale, Ill.: Southern Illinois University Press, 1986.

Gentry, Marshall Bruce, and William Stull, eds. *Conversations with Raymond Carver.* Jackson, Miss.: University Press of Mississippi, 1990.

Lohafer, Susan. *Coming to Terms with the Short Story.* Baton Rouge: Louisiana State University Press, 1983.

Lonnquist, Barbara. "Narrative Displacement and Literary Faith: Raymond Carver's Inheritance from Flannery O'Connor." In *Since Flannery O'Connor: Essays on the Contemporary American Short Story*, edited by Loren Logsdon and Charles W. Mayer. Macomb, Ill.: Western Illinois University Press, 1987.

McCaffery, Larry, ed. *Postmodern Fiction: A Bio-Bibliographical Guide.* Westport, Conn.: Greenwood Press, 1986.

Saltzman, Arthur M. *Understanding Raymond Carver.* Columbia, S.C.: University of South Carolina Press, 1988.

Smith, Allan Lloyd. "Brain Damage: The Word and the World in Postmodernist Writing." In *Contemporary American Fiction*, edited by Malcolm Bradbury and Sigmund Ro. London: Arnold, 1987.

Weaver, Gordon, ed. *The American Short Story, 1945–1980.* Boston: Twayne Publishers, 1983.

Articles in Periodicals

Applefield, David. "Fiction and America: Raymond Carver." *International Journal of Contemporary Writing and Art* 8–9 (1987–88): 6–15.

Atlas, James. "Less Is Less." *Atlantic Monthly*, June 1981, 96–98.

Barth, John. "A Few Words about Minimalism." *New York Times Book Review*, 28 December 1986, 1–2, 25.

Barthelme, Frederick. "On Being Wrong: Convicted Minimalist Spills Bean." *New York Times Book Review*, 3 April 1988, 1, 25–27.

Beattie, Ann. "Carver's *Furious Seasons.*" *Canto* 2, no. 2 (1978): 178–82.

Bell, Madison. "Less Is Less." *Harper's*, April 1986, 64–69.

Bosha, Francis J. "Raymond Carver's 'Cathedral.'" *Thought Currents in English Literature* 57 (1984): 149–51.

Boxer, David, and Cassandra Phillips. "*Will You Please Be Quite, Please?*: Voyeurism, Dissociation, and the Art of Raymond Carver." *Iowa Review* 10 (Summer 1979): 75–90.

Bugeja, Michael J. "Tarnish and Silver: An Analysis of Carver's *Cathedral.*" *South Dakota Review* 24, no. 3 (1986): 73–87.

Burford, Bill. "Everything Going Wrong." *Times Literary Supplement*, 17 February 1984, 159.

Campbell, Ewing. "Raymond Carver and the Literature of Subtraction." *Balcones Review* 1, no. 1 (1987): 69–71.

Carlin, Warren. "Just Talking: Raymond Carver's Symposium." *Cross Currents* 38, no. 1 (1988): 87–92.

Cochrane, Hamilton E. "'Taking the Cure': Alcoholism and Recovery in the Fiction of Raymond Carver." *University of Dayton Review* 20, no. 1 (Summer 1989): 79–88.

Cushman, Keith. "Blind, Intertextual Love: 'The Blind Man' and Raymond Carver's 'Cathedral.'" *Etudes Lawrenciennes* 3 (May 1988): 125–38.

Delbanco, Nicholas. "A Symposium on Contemporary American Fiction." *Michigan Quarterly Review* 26, no. 4 (1987): 679–758.

Dempsey, David. "Up, Up and Away with the Short Story." *Antioch Review* 42 (Spring 1984): 247–55.

Dunn, Robert. "Fiction That Shrinks from Life." *New York Times Book Review*, 30 June 1985, 1, 24–25.

Edwards, Thomas R. "The Short View: *Will You Please Be Quiet, Please?*" *New York Review of Books*, 1 April 1976, 35–36.

Facknitz, Mark. "Missing the Train: Raymond Carver's Sequel to John Cheever's 'The Five-Forty-Eight.'" *Studies in Short Fiction* 22, no. 3 (1985): 345–47.

———. "'The Calm,' 'A Small, Good Thing,' and 'Cathedral': Raymond Carver and the Rediscovery of Human Worth." *Studies in Short Fiction* 23, no. 3 (1986): 287–96.

———. "Raymond Carver and the Menace of Minimalism." *CEA Critic* 52, nos. 1–2 (Fall 1989-Winter 1990): 62–73.

Fisketjon, Gary. "Normal Nightmares." *Village Voice*, 18 September 1978, 132–34.

Flower, Dean. "Fiction Chronicle." *Hudson Review* 29 (Summer 1976): 270–72.

German, Norman, and Jack Bedell. "Physical and Social Laws in Ray Carver's 'Popular Mechanics.'" *Studies in Modern Fiction* 29 (Summer 1988): 257–60.

Goodheart, Eugene. "The Fiction of Raymond Carver." *Boston Review* 9, no. 1 (1984): 25.

Gorra, Michael. "Laughter and Bloodshed." *Hudson Review* 37 (Spring 1984): 151–64.

Grinnell, James W. *"Cathedral."* *Studies in Short Fiction* 21, (Winter 1984): 71–72.

Grumbach, Doris. "The Extra Skin That Language Can Give." *Georgia Review* 36 (Fall 1982): 668–74.

Henning, Barbara. "Minimalism and the American Dream: 'Shiloh' by Bobbie Ann Mason and 'Preservation' by Raymond Carver." *Modern Fiction Studies* 35 (1989): 689–98.

Herzinger, Kim. "Introduction: On the New Fiction." *Mississippi Review* 40–41 (Winter 1985): 7–22.

Hochschild, Adam. "Life through a Close-Up Lens." *Mother Jones*, October 1988, 50–51.

Houston, Robert. "A Stunning Inarticulateness." *Nation*, July 1981, 23–25.

Kellerman, Stewart. "Grace Has Come into My Life." *New York Times Book Review*, 15 May 1988, 40.

———. "For Raymond Carver, a Life Spent Battling Demons and Telling Stories." *New York Times*, 31 May 1988, 16.

———. "Raymond Carver, Writer and Poet of the Working Poor, Dies at Fifty." *New York Times*, 3 August 1988, B8.

Kubal, David. "Fiction Chronicle." *Hudson Review* 34 (Autumn 1981): 456–66.

LeClair, Thomas. "Fiction Chronicle—June 1981." *Contemporary Literature* 23 (Winter 1982): 83–91.

McInerney, Jay. "A Still, Small Voice." *New York Times Book Review*, 9 February 1986, 28.

Meyer, Adam. "Now You See Him, Now You Don't, Now You Do Again: The Evolution of Raymond Carver's Minimalism." *Critique* 30, no. 4 (Summer 1989): 239–51.

Moffett, Penelope. "Raymond Carver." *Publishers Weekly*, 27 May 1988, 42–44.

Newlove, Donald. *"What We Talk about When We Talk about Love."* *Saturday Review*, April 1981, 77.

O'Connell, Shaun. "Carver's Fires Burn with Magic." *Boston Globe*, 17 July 1983, sec. A, 55–56.

Pope, Dan. "The Post-Minimalist American Story or What Comes after Carver?" *Gettysburg Review* 1, no. 2 (1988): 332.

Queenan, Joe. "Character Assassins." *American Spectator* 21 (December 1988): 14–16.

Robinson, Marilynne. "Marriage and Other Astonishing Bonds." *New York Times Book Review*, 15 May 1988, 35, 40–41.

Rubins, Josh. "Small Expectations." *New York Review of Books,* 24 November 1983, 40–42.

Skenazy, Paul. "Life in Limbo: Ray Carver's Fiction." *Enclitic* 11, no. 1 (1988): 77–83.

Stewart, J. I. M. "Other Things." *London Review of Books,* 2–15 Feb. 1984, 16–17.

Stull, William. "Visions and Revisions." *Chariton Review* 10 (Spring 1984): 80–86.

———. "Beyond Hopelessville: Another Side of Raymond Carver," *Philological Quarterly* 64, no. 1 (1985): 1–15.

———. "Raymond Carver Remembered: Three Early Stories." *Studies in Short Fiction,* 25 (1988): 108–22.

VanderWeele, Michael. "Raymond Carver and the Language of Desire." *Denver Quarterly* 22, no. 1 (1987): 108–22.

Verley, Claudine. "Narration and Interiority in Raymond Carver's 'Where I'm Calling From.'" *Journal of the Short Story in English* 13 (1989): 91–102.

Weber, Bruce. "Raymond Carver: A Chronicler of Blue-Collar Despair." *New York Times Magazine,* 24 June 1984, 36–38, 42–46, 48–50.

Wolff, Geoffrey. "*Will You Please Be Quiet, Please?*" *New York Times Book Review,* 7 March 1976, 4–5.

Wolff, Tobias. "Raymond Carver: Had His Cake and Ate It Too." *Esquire,* September 1989, 240–48.

Index

The Author

Ewing Campbell is the author of *The Rincón Triptych*, *Piranesi's Dream*, and other works. He held a 1989 Fulbright lectureship in Argentina and a 1990 National Endowment for the Arts fellowship for fiction. He is an associate professor of English at Texas A&M University.

The Editor

Gordon Weaver earned his Ph.D. in English and creative writing at the University of Denver in 1970. He is professor of English at Oklahoma State University. He is the author of several novels, including *Count a Lonely Cadence, Give Him a Stone, Circling Byzantium*, and most recently *The Eight Corners of the World*. His short stories are collected in *The Entombed Man of Thule, Such Waltzing Was Not Easy, Getting Serious, Morality Play, A World Quite Round* and *Men Who Would Be Good* (1991). Recognition of his fiction includes the St. Lawrence Award for Fiction (1973), two National Endowment for the Arts fellowships (1974 and 1989), and the O. Henry First Prize (1979). He edited *The American Short Story, 1945–1980: A Critical History* and is currently editor of *Cimarron Review*. Married and the father of three daughters, he lives in Stillwater, Oklahoma.